GLORIOUS
FLOWERCRAFT

Glorious Flowercraft

A Sumptuous Workbook of Beautiful Floral
Creations for all Year Round

Pamela Westland
and
Marjie Lambert

THE
APPLE
PRESS

A QUINTET BOOK

Published by the Apple Press
6 Blundell Street
London N7

ISBN 1-85076-550-2

This book was designed and produced by
Quintet Publishing Limited
6 Blundell Street
London N7 9BH

Creative Director: Richard Dewing
Designer: Isobel Gillan
Project Editor: Anna Briffa
Editor: Sally Harper

Typeset in Great Britain by
Central Southern Typesetters, Eastbourne
Manufactured in Malaysia by C. H. Colour Scan Sdn. Bhd.
Printed in China by Leefung-Asco Printers Limited

The material in this publication previously appeared in:
Fragrant Crafts, Microwave Craft Magic,
Decorating with Dried Flowers,
Festive Garlands, Swags and Wreaths

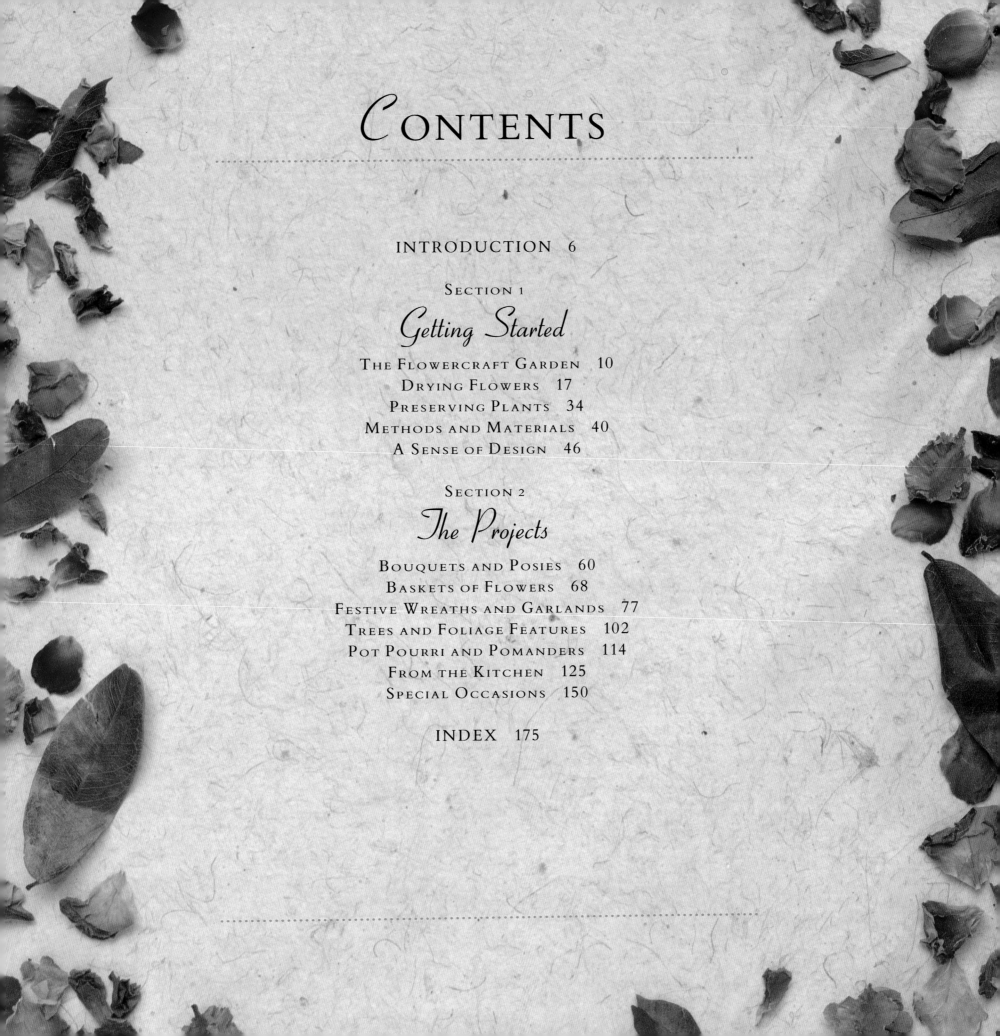

CONTENTS

INTRODUCTION

Think of the joy of the first daffodil of spring, or the glory of brilliantly coloured autumn leaves. They bring such pleasure, both in the garden and in your home. But how often have you cut a swathe of blooms, or bought a bunch of flowers from a market stall, only to find yourself needing inspiration when it comes to choosing a container for them or deciding how best to arrange them?

In this book, all the inspiration you need is provided. Not only are there ideas for combining different types of fresh flowers and foliage, there are also all the guidelines you will need for drying and preserving plant material, giving you the opportunity to enjoy arrangements in your home all year round.

Long before people "arranged" flowers in the way we now use the term, they made up garlands of flowers and leaves and festooned their homes as a symbol of good luck, victory, honour and worship. The practice of creating these decorations has survived the ages, although the symbolism has gradually changed. Garlands and bouquets are now appreciated for their purely decorative qualities, and set the scene for family celebrations and religious festivals alike. A garland of glossy evergreens outlining the fireplace at Christmas, a floral ribbon spanning a window, a swag of summery flowers draped across the bridal table at a wedding reception – the uses for flowers are as varied as your imagination. Choose from the luxury of fresh flowers in season; the long-lasting beauty of dried and preserved flowers, foliage and seedheads; the

wayward outlines of dried twigs and branches; the sheen of nuts and the heady aroma of herbs and spices – they all have a decorative part to play. The structures and shapes into which flowers and leaves can be arranged are many and varied, too: choose from baskets and bouquets, wreaths and garlands, indoor trees and pot pourris. Some are purely decorative, while others offer the aroma of flowers, herbs and spices as an added attraction.

Here, we have put a special emphasis on drying and preserving plant materials. This is a way of suspending nature, of holding leaves and blooms at the peak of their condition and in all their glorious array of colour. There is a special satisfaction in preserving floral material for yourself, although you may want to enhance your array of home-dried ingredients with the sort of exotic flowers and seedheads that are only available from specialist shops. Drying flowers and foliage is a simple matter, and at its easiest level just involves hanging them in a warm, airy place.

Whether you want to create floral arrangements to set the scene for a special occasion, or simply to bring natural beauty indoors, you will find ideas throughout this book to delight and inspire you. In the first section, the ways and means of flowercraft are explained, from growing plants especially for drying through to choosing the right containers and arrangements to suit the setting you have in mind, taking into account the shapes and colours that will look best in your own home. There are practical explanations of the different ways you can preserve flowers and foliage (including the use of a microwave), and a guide to the tools and materials you will need to create floral arrangements.

Having dealt with the general guidelines, we get down to specifics: in the second section of this book is a range of projects that use fresh and dried flowers, foliage, nuts and herbs. Step-by-step photographs show how each design is put together, with a photo-graph of the finished result so that you can easily choose the type of arrangement to suit your needs. You should not feel constrained by the suggestions we make and the flowers and leaves we have used. You will soon see how easy it is to adapt each design to your own requirements, preferences and colour schemes, using our suggestions as a spring-board to your own creative and artistic flair.

BELOW A basket of dried flowers and grasses is a thoughtful way to show your appreciation to your host – but it may be tempting to keep it yourself! Here, rosebuds, helichrysums (strawflowers), sea lavender, hydrangeas, statice and larkspur are set off with grasses and a paper bow as the finishing touch.

GETTING STARTED

The wonderful thing about decorating with flowers is that it is a quick and infinitely adaptable way of adding a personal signature to your home. We are all surrounded by plant material that can be used fresh or dried to create any number of arrangements. If you have a garden then, as we shall see, the scope is immense, from border flowers and herbs to twigs and branches and even vegetables. If you have access to a friend's or neighbour's garden then you might be allowed to rescue some seedheads that might otherwise have been consigned to the rubbish heap: lupins, for example, which look like silvery grey velvet pods, and lavatera (mallow), which are like silver stars.

If you have bought an impulse bunch of flowers you might decide to dry one or two of them and slowly build up a dried collection – daffodils dried in dessicant, or a stem of mimosa dried in a container, perhaps. And if you have been given a florists' bouquet or a spray of flowers, you might decide to dry some of the flowers as a lasting memento.

On a walk in the country or in a wood, you might find a treasure trove of items to arrange fresh or dry – cones, nuts, grasses and seedheads, wild oats, gnarled twigs and pieces of wood in interesting shapes. Remember that wild flowers are protected by law, and it may be illegal to pick them: if you are in doubt, play safe and do not pick any.

The first chapters in this section of the book deal mainly with the art of preserving plant materials. You may choose to follow the most straightforward techniques, such as air drying flowers; or you might become more involved in flowercraft and experiment with a full range of methods. Whichever path you follow, the chapter on flowercraft and design will give you all the advice you need on making the most of the arrangements you create.

LEFT *Herbs and flowers hanging in bunches on a rack can be dried outdoors on a dry day, but they should not be left in strong sunlight.*

THE FLOWERCRAFT GARDEN

Any garden can yield a wealth of flowers and plants for fresh arrangements or for drying. Even the smallest courtyard or patio will probably already offer flowers and foliage in many shapes, colours and textures that can be used to ornament your home in a variety of imaginative ways.

With a little forethought, you can maximize the harvest from your garden. Firstly you might choose to arrange your garden to make it easier to collect the cut flowers, and plant the sorts of flowers, shrubs and trees that will be of most use to you in arrangements. Once again, you do not need an enormous area to do this: even in the smallest container gardens, there is scope for variety. When it comes to harvesting plant materials, some forward planning will help you to pick flowers at their peak; this is particularly important if you intend to dry the plant material. Timing is all-important. Not only must the season be right, but the time of day that you gather your plants matters as well.

You can easily prolong the life of your flowers simply by treating them well. Like all living things, flowers respond to a little care and attention. Remember that flowers and leaves are traumatized by being removed from their food source; you can help them recover from the shock by keeping them moist and unbruised.

LEFT *With such a diverse range of colours and forms available, you will be able to use dried flower arrangements to suit virtually any decor, and to complement any room in your house.*

GROWING PLANTS FOR DRYING

One of the greatest joys of owning a garden is harvesting flowers, seedheads and other plant materials for fresh arrangements or for drying. There is a special thrill in going from plant to plant, a basket over your arm, gathering flowers which, after a simple drying process, you can enjoy in arrangements for months to come.

You may like to gather flowers from here and there in the borders and beds: a stem or two of midnight-blue delphinium captured at the peak of perfection, a few rosebuds, a bunch of pink and white clarkia, a handful of poppy or rue seedheads, whatever you have. Or, if you are already a dried flower enthusiast, you may perhaps have a small area, like a kitchen garden, set aside to grow flowers specially for drying.

It is a good idea to do this, for a number of reasons. For one thing, having a dried flower patch enables you to grow flowers in rows, maximizing the use of the space and facilitating harvest. It is much easier to keep an eye on a row of flowers, gathering a few each day as they reach prime condition, than it is if they are scattered around the garden among other plants. Not only that, you can grow flowers for drying regardless of their size and scale in relation to your borders and beds, and regardless of their overall visual appeal. No plant is too tall and unwieldy nor too small and insignificant to grow in a "working patch", whereas it might look out of place in a mixed border.

If you do consider planting a dried flower patch, this is the place to grow all the everlastings, the flowers that dry to a papery crispness on the plant and form the foundation of many a dried flower collection. These include helichrysums (strawflowers) in shades from palest peach to deepest crimson; winged everlasting with its yellow-domed, white daisy-like flowers; sunray (swan river) everlasting in deep pink and purest white; and statice in all its artist's-palette range of lours. Try to find space, too, for the yellow-flowered silver-leaved (white-leaf) everlasting, for feverfew with its tiny white domes of flowers, for love-in-a-mist which dries at both the baby-blue flowering stage and the seedhead stage, and for the delicate bush-like plants of gypsophila (baby's breath) in both white and pink. On a larger scale you might like to include a plant or two of golden rod (a large subject with small-scale design potential); tansy with its generous clusters of tiny golden flowers; and achillea (yarrow) in varieties which provide you with flat-topped clusters of yellow, cream, pink and white flowers, all excellent candidates for drying.

ABOVE *Tiny white yellow-centre feverfew will provide a delicate touch to dried flower designs.*

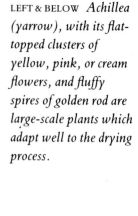

LEFT & BELOW *Achillea (yarrow), with its flat-topped clusters of yellow, pink, or cream flowers, and fluffy spires of golden rod are large-scale plants which adapt well to the drying process.*

FAR LEFT *Delphiniums and the smaller larkspur are handsome border plants, much used in dried flower decorations. They should be harvested for drying when the topmost flowers are still in bud.*

Some plants are worth growing, either in a working patch or in a border, for their decorative seedheads. These include poppy, honesty, teasel and rue, which all have definite design appeal when mixed with other dried materials.

Make room, too, either in your working patch or a corner of the garden, for ornamental grasses, which make such a pretty neutral foil to more showy and colourful plant materials. You can buy packets of mixed ornamental grass seed which include quaking grass, hare's-tail grass and many others that have an attractive part to play in floral designs.

Do not overlook the vegetable garden in your quest for suitable materials for drying. Onion and garlic seedheads, chive and marjoram flowers, corn-on-the-cob heads, sorrel

ABOVE *Decorative seedheads, such as teasels, provide neutral tones, bold shapes and strong textures to a design.*

seeds and globe artichokes – as varied a group of plant materials as it would be possible to imagine – all dry well and extend the range of your collection.

If your dried flower garden is confined to a small patio, a balcony or even just a couple of windowboxes, there is still scope for variety. You might have tubs of mop-headed or lace-cap hydrangeas, which dry well by air drying; lady's mantle, with its fluffy clusters of lime-green flowers; miniature roses, one of the most charming of dried materials; and pink and blue cornflowers, which retain their brilliant colours perfectly. All the everlastings can be planted in pots, tubs and troughs, and are good value; they have an extended flowering period, providing colour and interest long before they are ready for harvesting.

HARVESTING
~

Just as it is with cereal and other food crops, so it is with flowers and other materials for drying. If they are to dry satisfactorily, retain their form and colour, and give pleasure for many months to come, they must be harvested when conditions are just right and they are in peak condition.

Naturally the weather plays a key role; it can be very frustrating to see flowers just becoming ready to cut when torrential rain arrives. It is important to gather flowers and seedheads when they are absolutely dry and carrying no excess moisture. This means harvesting them on a dry day and at certain times of the day, once the early morning dew has dried off and before the evening dew settles. When harvesting flowers (it does not matter about seedheads) it is advisable to avoid midday, when the sun is at its highest, since the flowers tend to wilt rather than begin the drying process slowly and surely. This means, then, that the ideal time for your floral harvest is mid-morning and mid- to late afternoon.

Capturing the various types of flowers at the right stage for drying calls for a fine degree of judgement. Those for air drying need to be cut before they are fully opened. In the case of long spike-like flowers, such as delphinium, the smaller larkspur and clarkia, this means gathering them when a few of the flowers at the base of the stem are fully opened, those higher up are partly opened and the topmost ones are still in bud. Roses are a special case: you can cut them in tight bud, when they will dry readily, retaining their closed, tightly-furled form, or when the buds have started to unfurl but before they are fully open.

If you plan to dry flowers in a desiccant (see pages 20 to 22) you can harvest them at a later stage, just as they become fully open. Leave them a day or two later, though, and you might find the results disappointing.

Gathering plant materials at just the right stage of their development calls for another piece of careful timing. If you are planning a one-day design to decorate a festive or party scene, then you will want the flowers to be almost at the peak of their maturity; almost,

LEFT *The vegetable garden can be a rich source of materials for drying. Chives, with their pink, dome-shaped flowerheads, are a member of the onion family and dry well.*

BELOW *Lavender is an easy and decorative plant to grow in casual clumps, or in pots and troughs. Lavender spires retain their heady scent when dried and are ideal for use in aromatic dried flower designs for the bedroom; or simply crush the flowers and add to a pot pourri blend.*

but not quite. Flowers that are fully developed (cabbagy, full-blown roses are an example) are also on the verge of their downward spiral, in both visual and development terms, and are likely to wilt much more quickly than ones that are harvested a day or so earlier.

When flowers are intended for a longer lasting arrangement (say, for a fresh-flower ring to decorate the table throughout the long Easter weekend), then it is advisable to select flowers which are far from being fully open. In this way you will not only ensure that they "stay the course", but you will have the pleasure of watching them develop gradually from day to day.

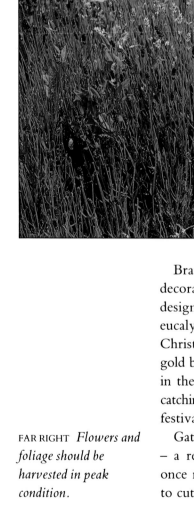

Branches of preserved leaves have a highly decorative role to play in wreath and garland designs, from short snippings of frosty-green eucalyptus blended with wintry materials in a Christmas table wreath to swathes of copper-gold beech leaves wired with fruit and flowers in the burnished shades of autumn, an eye-catching design for a Thanksgiving or harvest festival celebration.

Gathering deciduous leaves for preserving – a reassuringly simple process – requires, once more, sensitive timing. It is important to cut the branches when the leaves are fully

FAR RIGHT *Flowers and foliage should be harvested in peak condition.*

HARVESTING HINTS

When harvesting leaves and flowers for drying, here are a few tips worth remembering.

- Flowers should be not quite at their peak of bloom.

- Flowers in full bloom often lose their petals during drying.

- Do not pick flowers for drying while they are still dewy or wet from rain; they should be dry.

- Or, let flowers stand in a vase, if necessary, until dry.

- Zinnias, chrysanthemums and daisies are excellent flowers for beginners, as are flat leaves like maple and elm.

mature and while the sap is still rising in the plants. Cut the stems too early in the season, when the leaves are still young and tender (and this limitation applies to evergreens too), and the foliage is likely to wilt during the preserving process. Cut them too late in their development cycle, when the sap has stopped rising and the leaves are beginning to lose their natural moisture and change colour, and they will not be able to take up the preserving solution successfully. That is the bad news. The good news is that you can harvest branches throughout the whole summer, processing a few at a time, and build up an entire collection of russet, bronze and copper-coloured leaves to twist, weave and bind into long-lasting decorations around the home or in a church.

CARING FOR FRESHLY CUT FLOWERS
~

As we have seen, the transition from growing plant to design component represents a quantum leap for both flowers and leaves. To minimize the shock of being severed from their food source, stems must be put into intensive care almost from the moment of harvesting. In effect, this simply means that they must be given a good long drink of water and left in a cool place for several hours – overnight if that is convenient – before being arranged.

When you are harvesting plant materials on a hot and sultry day, it is advisable to take a bucket or bowl of water with you, strip off any leaves that would come below the waterline and place the stems directly into it. This may not have quite the romantic appeal of wandering from plant to plant with a rustic flower basket over your arm, but it will pay dividends in terms of longevity and freshness of appearance. If you plan to gather plant materials in the wild or from a friend's garden some way away, be prepared to wrap the

RIGHT *Flowers can be revived instantly by cutting a piece off the end of each stem at a sharp angle and placing them in a container of water.*

LEFT *You can have the best of both worlds by combining the aesthetic pleasure of gathering flowers and foliage in a rustic basket with the practical precaution of putting the stems straight into water. A bowl of water in this small willow basket gives instant refreshment to variegated mint, cornflowers, nasturtiums and red campion (Lychnis coronaria).*

BELOW *As tulips have a reputation for drooping, they would benefit from being tightly wrapped in newspaper before being immersed in water.*

stems in a bundle of damp tissues or a wad of cotton wool, and – especially in the case of small and delicate wild flowers – enclose them completely in a polythene bag. The condensation that will form inside will become a valuable moisture source and help to keep the flowers fresh throughout the journey.

Flowers that you buy from a florist or market will already have endured one journey since they were harvested, and may well have another before you get them home. Even if, as a result, they do look a little jaded there is no need to despair. Cut a short piece – about 1in (2.5cm) – at a sharp angle from the end of each stem and stand them in a deep container of water to revive them. Flowers that have a reputation for drooping (ranunculus, tulips and roses, for example) benefit from being tightly wrapped in a newspaper, right around the bunch of stems and up past the flower heads, before being immersed.

Once the flowers and leaves have been revived, take a critical look at each stem – your last chance to do so before you spend time and trouble arranging them or preserving them for later use. Discard any flowers or foliage sprays that are still droopy or wilted; they are beyond recall. Look carefully at the others: it may be that a little cosmetic treatment can rescue many an unpromising-looking specimen. Pick off any discoloured outer petals, of roses, for example, until you re-create an unblemished bloom. Do not be tempted to waste time and space by drying imperfect materials. Damaged petals are likely to rot and could then affect other materials around them. Snip off torn or insect-damaged leaves from otherwise healthy sprays; any resulting lack of symmetry will be imperceptible in a finished design. And snip off any bare stem ends which may have carried the earliest-flowering blooms. Natural as these are on the plant, barren stems take on a most unattractive appearance in a design.

Strip off all lower leaves from flower stems, especially those that would be trapped by the string when tying them in bunches. Crunched up and without a free circulation of air, the leaves would rot and affect the rest of the plant material.

DRYING FLOWERS

Capture the pleasures of your garden for long-term enjoyment by drying a selection of plant materials. By drying the choicest blooms, leaves, herbs and seeds, you can soon build up a store of decorative and fragrant materials full of evocative memories.

Many leaves and flowers may be dried by the simplest and most seemingly natural method of all – by hanging them in bunches in a warm, dry, airy place, a process known as air drying. Other plants, which lose their form or substance by this method, may be dried in a desiccant over a long period. For quicker results, the microwave oven has revolutionized the flower drying process: your blooms and stems can be ready to use in a matter of minutes. Because microwave drying has become so popular over the past few years, the different uses of the microwave oven are discussed here in some detail.

No matter which approach to drying you use, no particular expertise is needed. The following pages explain how to choose the method that is right for the type of plant material you wish to preserve, and give useful tips that will help you to achieve the best possible results. At the end of this chapter you will find tables for ready reference to the right technique for drying a wide range of herbs, seeds, leaves and flowers.

RIGHT Contradictory though it may seem, immersing the stems in a small amount of water is one way to dry hydrangea heads and gypsophila (baby's breath).

AIR DRYING
~

Air drying is the simplest and the most widely used method of drying plant material. All you need is space in a dry, warm room with a free circulation of air. The temperature should not fall below 50°F (10°C) and there should be no induced moisture in the air. This rules out a steamy kitchen, utility room or bathroom. An airing cupboard, the space over or around a central heating boiler, a spare bedroom, an attic or loft or, in summer time, a shed or garage may all be suitable. Bear in mind that plant materials can look highly decorative throughout the drying process and you might add the sitting room or dining room to the list of possibilities.

RIGHT *A cool collection of materials air-dried by hanging. There is quaking grass, hare's-tail grass, silver-leaved (white-leaf) everlasting and lady's mantle.*

Plant materials can be air dried by one of several methods. Plants can be hung individually or in bunches, stood upright in a roomy container, laid flat on shelves or racks, placed in boxes or wound around a horizontal pole. Some plants will dry successfully by only one method and others offer a choice.

Whatever the method, it is important that air can circulate around the materials as they dry, since air is the only drying medium employed. This means making up small bunches with the flower heads staggered and separated from each other, hanging some large stems individually, or choosing a wide-necked container so that stems can fan out away from each other, allowing plenty of space all around them as they dry.

To dry materials by hanging, gather the stems into bunches, just a few specimens in each, and tie them with raffia or twine. Hang the bunches upside-down on wire coat-hangers, on strings or rods suspended across a room corner, on coat-hooks (as long as the materials hang away from the wall surface) or on clothes airing racks.

CREATING COLOUR

You do not have to limit yourself to the colours nature provides. Some flowers, including gypsophila (baby's breath), helichrysums (strawflowers), hydrangeas, achillea (yarrow) and golden rod, can be coloured easily with fabric dye. The most common method is to dissolve powdered dye in boiling water and immerse the dried flowers for 10 minutes or longer, or you can follow the directions on the dye package. Some items, including holly leaves, eucalyptus, nuts and pine cones, take on a new beauty when coloured with spray paint – particularly silver, gold and white.

ABOVE *Linseed, sea lavender and a selection of grasses can also be dried by standing upright, well spread out, in a container.*

grass. Other plants – although it sounds a contradiction in terms – may be dried by standing in water. These include hydrangea, mimosa, gypsophila (baby's breath), cornflower and pearl everlasting. Pour about 2in (5cm) of water into a wide-necked container such as a casserole dish or large preserving jar and stand the stems so that the ends are under water. As the stems gradually absorb the water it evaporates and the plant material naturally dries.

Some plant materials dry most successfully when placed flat on absorbent paper on racks or shelves. All grasses give good results in this way. Dock and sorrel seedheads, giant hogweed and lavender are others that do well. Place the materials in a single layer on the paper and turn them carefully every day or so, so that each part of the plant material is uppermost in turn.

Mushrooms and other fungi can be dried by hanging (thread a piece of string through them and hang the string across the airing cupboard) or by being placed on absorbent paper. Make sure that the fungus is dry before you start the dehydration process. If it is the slightest bit moist it will rot. Check caps and stems for insects, too. It is worth noting that the warm air that is needed for drying provides just the right breeding conditions for all kinds of creeping creatures.

Pine and fir cones, a harvest you can gather during a walk in the woods, dry well by being placed on a shelf or in a box in a dry, warm room. Try to gather a collection of different sizes and shapes so that you have enough for designs of all kinds. Horse chestnuts, or conkers, another treasure from the countryside, dry well in boxes and make glossy highlights, especially in winter arrangements.

Climbing plants dry most attractively if you wind them around a pole suspended horizontally, perhaps across a room corner. Once dry, these twisty-twirly stems are most effective if they are used to outline an arch.

All the everlasting flowers, including helichrysums (strawflowers), winged everlasting and statice, may be dried in this way. Other candidates include materials made up of a mass of tiny flowers or florets which, as they dry, shrivel almost imperceptibly and retain their original form. Among the flowers in this category are hydrangea, golden rod, tansy, achillea (yarrow), mimosa, lady's mantle, larkspur and clarkia; and the seedheads include poppy, love-in-a-mist, mallow, lupin and rue. Chinese lanterns, most brilliant of all seedheads, are stripped of all their leaves and dried by hanging, and so are rosebuds, stripped of only their lower leaves. Rose leaves closer to the flower head furl attractively as they dry and become a feature of the dried plant material.

Very few leaves can be dried successfully by air drying, though sage is an exception. Both green and purple sage leaves furl most attractively in the hang-drying process and are a useful addition to a collection.

Plant materials which can be dried upright in a dry container include sea lavender, feverfew, bulrushes, corn-on-the cob heads, globe artichokes, onion seedheads and pampas

BELOW *Some of the stateliest of dried materials – bulrushes, pampas grass and hogweed – are dried upright in a container.*

WIRING STEMS BEFORE DRYING

Some flowers may need to have false wire stems attached before they are dried. These include helichrysums (strawflowers), which frequently snap from their brittle stems, and multiflora roses, which grow in clusters on short stems.

• To wire helichrysums (strawflowers), push a medium-gauge stub wire up through the base of the flower and out through the top. Bend over a small hook, like a hairpin, and pull it down into the flower centre where it will be concealed.

• To wire roses, place stub wire against the short stem and bind the two together, using silver roll wire or fuse wire. Take the binding wire down beyond the stem, twisting it until it is secure.

• Hang the wired flowers in bunches to dry, easing out the wire stems so that the flower heads are not touching each other.

• Once the flowers are dried, the false stems can be covered with gutta-percha binding tape to conceal them.

above a door architrave.

The time taken to air dry flowers and other plant materials will vary considerably according to the moisture content of the materials and the temperature and humidity of the room. In a warm airing cupboard a stem of delphinium could be dry in two or three days. In a cooler shed or garage it could take eight to ten days to reach the stage when it is safe from developing mould. Test your materials every two or three days. Flowers, leaves and seedheads are ready when they sound and feel as crisp as tissue paper.

DESICCANT DRYING
~

If air drying is considered to be the completely natural way to dry flowers, seedheads and other materials, then drying in a desiccant, or a drying agent, may be thought of as the more scientific means. Instead of relying on a free circulation of air, this method employs dry granules or powder to draw out the moisture from the flower petals. It is suitable for a wide range of flower types and may be used to preserve fully opened flowers.

The principle is to cover every part of the surface area of every petal with the drying agent, which then draws out the moisture evenly and completely. The story goes that the method was first discovered several centuries ago by a cook on a large English estate. She is said to have buried rose petals in powdered sugar to scent it, ready to make delicate confections. When she came to remove the petals, she found that they had retained their colour, form and shape perfectly and were, quite simply, dried versions of their former selves. And so a new technique was born!

In fact, powdered sugar is not now recommended as a drying agent, as it has a tendency to become sticky as it absorbs moisture. The most popular and effective desiccant is silica gel crystals which you can buy in some chemist shops. They are available in standard white or in a colour-indicated form: blue crystals which turn pink as they absorb moisture and become damp. You need to grind them down to at least half of their original size, using a pestle and mortar or a blender. Silica dust, inevitable when you are pouring silica gel, can irritate your nose and throat, so work in a well-ventilated room. You may want to use an inexpensive filter mask over your nose and mouth, the type you would use to avoid breathing dust created by sanding plaster, available at hardware stores.

Drying Flowers in Desiccant

1 A shallow layer of ground silica gel crystals forms a base for cosmos and nasturtium, the first stage in the desiccant drying process.

2 The crystals are sprinkled over the flowers to cover them, and then the box is covered with the airtight lid. The flowers should be dry in two to three days.

Other suitable drying agents are borax and alum powders, both available from some chemists, and dry silver sand. The powders may be used alone but they tend to cling to the dried petals, leaving a white film, which is difficult to brush off. It is best to use three parts powder mixed with two parts silver sand. The sand may be used alone for larger plant materials such as mop-head chrysanthemums and dahlias, but never for small flowers, since its weight would crush them.

To dry flowers in this way, sprinkle a thin layer of the desiccant, about 1cm (½in), in the base of a biscuit tin that has a tight-fitting lid. Place the flowers on the drying agent, spaced well apart and not touching each other, sprinkle on more desiccant so that it fills any hollows in the flowers – the trumpets of daffodils for example – and brush it lightly to cover all the petals. A small camel-hair brush is most suitable for this delicate task. When all the flowers are covered, sprinkle on a thin layer of the desiccant, put on the lid and set the tin aside where it need not be moved.

If you use silica gel crystals, check the flowers after two to three days and remove them as soon as they are dry. Leaving them in the crystals for too long makes them impracticably brittle. If you use a chemical and sand mixture, check the flowers after about six days. Carefully remove the lid, taking care not to shake up the contents of the tin. Brush aside the top layer and check one of the flowers for dryness.

When the flowers are dry, carefully remove them from the desiccant – tweezers are useful for this – and brush away any clinging powder or crystals with the camel-hair brush.

The purchase of any of these desiccants can be a once-in-a-while event since they can be used over and over again. After using the drying agent, sieve it to remove any plant particles that may have become detached, then spread it on baking trays and dry it in a low-temperature oven, until the colour-indicated silica gel crystals return to blue. Allow the desiccant to cool, then store it in an airtight tin or jar.

The desiccant drying method is suitable for preserving composite flowers such as daisy, marguerite daisy, spray chrysanthemum, gerbera (Transvaal daisy) and marigold; "hollow" flowers such as daffodil, narcissus, lily, orchid and freesia; flat-faced flowers such as buttercup, camellia, anemone and pansy; and a host of others. You can dry separate flowers from a stem of delphinium; complete stems of lily-of-the-valley and grape hyacinth; tightly clustered flowers such as ranunculus and zinnia; or fully opened roses and peonies – the list is endless, and is limited only by the amount of desiccant, space, time and plant material you have available.

To prepare flowers for desiccant drying you need to cut off all or most of the stem, and, while the flower is still supple, insert or wire on a short length of stub wire, the foundation for a false stem to be bound on once the flower has been dried. See page 20 for the method.

Once they are dried, flowers can be stored between tissues in a box or drawer. And once they have been bound on to a full-length wire stem they can be stored upright, the stems inserted in a piece of dry foam and angled so that the flowers do not touch or crush each other.

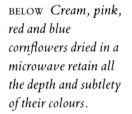

BELOW *Cream, pink, red and blue cornflowers dried in a microwave retain all the depth and subtlety of their colours.*

MICROWAVE DRYING
~

Air drying and desiccant drying are traditional methods of preserving flowers which have been practised for generations. Now a new method has come on the scene: drying in a microwave oven. This is a technique to experiment with, taking snippings of flowers and foliage and testing to see how well they preserve. In general terms, the method is suitable for small sprays of many of the plant materials that can be preserved by air drying, but is not suitable for composite or "hollow" flowers, which just collapse.

Your garden is probably full of flowers you can dry in the microwave. Some of the most popular flowers are prime candidates for micro drying: zinnias, daisies, roses, chrysanthemums, hydrangeas, gypsophila (baby's breath), primroses, marigolds, calendulas and helichrysums (strawflowers) are among them. Boughs of silver-dollar eucalyptus are eye-catching additions; autumn leaves add

LEFT *Displayed here are the basic ingredients needed for microwave drying. The white granules in the glass bowl are silica gel, the substance thought to be the most effective drying agent, which can also be used over and over.*

COLOUR AND THE MICROWAVE

Some flowers hold their colour better than others when dried in a microwave. The brightest colours are most likely to stay true after drying. Others fade or develop a brown undertone. My marigolds and calendulas kept their bright yellows and oranges, while my gold chrysanthemums turned bronze, and the purple chrysanthemums took on a brown tinge. My deep-pink and white primroses turned a lovely shade of lavender, while the white stayed pure. Most white flowers turned to cream or got brown around the edges. White delphinium turned light blue, but white daisies, candytuft and dogwood stayed white.

wonderful colour to all sorts of arrangements; and herbs also add visual interest – the pale green of sage, the purplish-red seedheads of oregano, tiny purple flowers on rosemary sprigs, the immature seedheads and feathery fronds of anise are but a few examples.

Roadside and wildland weeds usually not noticed – wild wheat and oats, sorrel, pampas grass, thistle and papyrus – can also be dried using the microwave.

The long stems of sorrel are too big for many ovens. Bright red berries often burst in microwaves, and should, instead, be hung to dry for at least a week in a cool, dry, well-ventilated place. Fleshy flowers, such as magnolias and hyacinth, generally dry poorly. Pansy flowers are something of a hit-and-miss affair, giving passable results most times. If they emerge looking slightly crumpled, they can be coaxed back to their pristine shape by being pressed under a heavy weight for an hour or so.

THE OPEN METHOD OF DRYING HERBS, LEAVES AND FLOWERS

Herbs, leaves and flowers can also be dried in the microwave without any drying agent. This method is prefereable in certain circumstances, such as when you're drying flowers for pot pourri, or herbs for a wreath, and may want to use the herbs in cooking later. It is also better to dry unopened rosebuds this way, since the silica will not penetrate to the bud's centre, and aggravates uneven drying.

When the open method is used, it is better to dry the herbs in batches, one type at a time, since most require different drying times. Cooking times vary from 4 to 6 minutes for fragile leaves like basil, up to 10 minutes for sage and rosemary.

The disadvantage of the open method is that it takes two to four times as long as the silica gel method. Also, the flowers tend to lose their shape or become badly shrivelled, making this method best for herbs and some leaves.

BELOW Some herbs, leaves and flowers can be dried without any drying agent but they need to be dried in small batches and one type at a time. The disadvantage is that this method takes longer than if silica gel is used.

Microwave drying is not a difficult or expensive process, especially if you cut flowers from your garden and scavenge roadside weeds and grasses. But start slowly and experiment with different techniques and microwave settings until you develop a good sense of what works in your microwave. Also, remember dried leaves and flowers are brittle, and your fingers are apt to be clumsy until you get the hang of wiring them – you will discard quite a few broken flowers and leaves in the beginning.

Trim off all but an inch or so of the stem before drying. (Most dried flower stems are extremely fragile and crumble away when you handle them.)

You may also use cornmeal or borax or a mixture of the two, but they take roughly 50 per cent longer to dry than silica gel. Cornmeal and borax can be reused, although they do not last as long as silica gel. Cooking times vary widely, depending on the type of microwave, the type and quantity of flowers, and the heat retained by silica gel in continuous use. Experiment until you get consistent results. I use a Medium–Low setting of 40 per cent power, but that setting will not work in all microwaves. The chart on page 29 to 30 will give you some guidelines for cooking times. Then, just as food cooked in a microwave oven continues cooking for a few minutes after it comes out of the oven, the flower-drying process continues after they are removed from the oven. Let flowers and leaves sit in the silica gel for at least 10 minutes or more, depending on size.

ABOVE This beautiful microwaved cream rose shows the positive effect the drying process can have on the colours of the plant materials.

Drying Herbs in the Microwave

1 Pour a 1in (2.5cm) layer of silica gel into a microwave-safe dish. Place a herb sprig, such as rosemary, on the granules. Gently spoon additional silica over the herb until it is completely covered.

2 Place the dish or dishes into the microwave. Cooking times vary widely, so experiment until you get consistent results. Once the dishes are out of the oven, leave the herbs undisturbed for at least 10 minutes.

3 Carefully pour some of the silica gel off the herbs until they can be easily removed. Using a small, soft paintbrush, gently brush off silica granules; stubborn granules will probably fall off on their own later. Set the herbs on a wire cooling rack until ready for use.

YOU WILL NEED

Silica gel

Microwave-safe dish

Small spoon

Wire cooling rack

Selection of fresh herbs

Drying Flowers in the Microwave

YOU WILL NEED

Silica gel

Microwave-safe dish

Florists' scissors

Small spoon

Small, soft paintbrush

Wire cooling rack

Selection of fresh flowers

1 Pour a 1in (2.5cm) layer of silica gel into a microwave-safe dish.

2 Trim off all but about 1in (2.5cm) of the stem from the flowers to be dried.

3 Insert the stems into the silica, then the flower heads. If the silica is not sufficiently deep to support the flowers, spoon additional silica around their bases.

4 Gently spoon additional silica gel over flower tops until they are completely covered.

5 Place the dish into the microwave. Cooking times vary widely, see pages 29 to 30 for guidelines. Once the dish is out of the microwave, leave the flowers undisturbed for at least 10 minutes.

6 Carefully pour some of the silica gel off the flowers, until they can be removed quite easily.

7 Using a small, soft paintbrush, gently brush off silica granules, stubborn granules will probably fall off on their own later. Petals and leaves are very brittle at this point, and are easily broken by the brushing motion. Set the flowers on a wire cooling rack to protect the shapes.

POSITIONING FLOWERS IN SILICA GEL

There are two ways to position flowers in silica gel. All open-faced flowers such as pansies, carnations, roses and daffodils should be placed upright in the silica to ensure that the flower is covered inside and outside with silica. Imagine it as a cup that needs to be filled. All sprays such as statice, lily-of-the-valley and jasmine should be laid horizontally in the silica gel.

Drying Leaves in the Microwave

1 Pour a 1in (2.5cm) layer of silica gel into a microwave-safe dish. Lay the leaves on the granules. Gently spoon additional silica gel over the leaves until they are completely covered.

YOU WILL NEED

Silica gel

Microwave-safe dish

Small spoon

Small, soft paintbrush

Wire cooling rack

Leaves

2 Place the dish into the microwave. Cooking times vary; see pages 29 to 30 for guidelines. Once the dish is out of the oven, let the leaves sit undisturbed for at least 10 minutes.

4 Using a small, soft paintbrush, gently brush off silica granules; stubborn granules will probably fall off on their own later. Set the leaves on a wire cooling rack to protect their shape until ready to use.

3 Carefully pour some of the silica gel off the leaves, until they can be easily removed.

Drying Flowers

Here are a few examples of times that worked for me, using the silica gel method. All were heated at the Medium–Low power (40 per cent) setting (280 watts in a 700–watt oven), and were left to stand undisturbed for at least 10 minutes after they came out of the microwave.

FLOWERS	QUANTITY	BOX SIZE	AMOUNT OF SILICA GEL	TIME
ACHILLEA (YARROW)	3 stems	4 × 4in (10 × 10cm)	4in (10cm)	3½ minutes
ARTEMISIA	4 stems	10 × 6in (25 × 15cm)	3in (8cm)	3 minutes
ASTER	5 asters, 2in (5cm) diameter	10 × 6in (25 × 15cm)	3in (8cm)	4½ minutes
CAMPION *(SILENE)*	4 stems	10 × 6in (25 × 15cm)	3in (8cm)	3½ minutes
CANDYTUFT	4 stems	10 × 6in (25 × 15cm)	3in (8cm)	3½ minutes
CARNATION	3 carnations, 1½in (4cm) diameter	4 × 4in (10 × 10cm)	3in (8cm)	3½ minutes
CHINESE LANTERN*	6 lanterns, cut open	10 × 6in (25 × 15cm)	3in (8cm)	4½ minutes
CHRYSANTHEMUM	3 button mums 8 mums	4 × 4in (10 × 10cm) 10 × 6in (25 × 15cm)	3in (8cm) 3in (8cm)	5 minutes 7½ minutes
CORNFLOWER	4 cornflowers	4 × 4in (10 × 10cm)	3in (8cm)	2½ minutes
COSMOS	3 cosmos	4 × 4in (10 × 10cm)	3in (8cm)	2 minutes
DAISY	5 Gloriosa daisies	10 × 6in (25 × 15cm)	3in (8cm)	3½ minutes
GLOBE AMARANTH	4 stems	4 × 4in (10 × 10cm)	4in (10cm)	4 minutes
GOLDEN ROD	4 stems	10 × 6in (25 × 15cm)	3in (8cm)	3½ minutes
GYPSOPHILA (BABY'S BREATH)	2 stems	10 × 6in (25 × 15cm)	3in (8cm)	3 minutes
HELICHRYSUM (STRAWFLOWER)	3 strawflowers 8 strawflowers	4 × 4in (10 × 10cm) 10 × 6in (25 × 15cm)	3in (8cm) 3in (8cm)	3½ minutes 6 minutes
HYDRANGEA	1 cluster	4 × 4in (10 × 10cm)	4in (10cm)	4 minutes
LADY'S MANTLE	2 stems	10 × 6in (25 × 15cm)	3in (8cm)	3½ minutes
LARKSPUR	4 stems	10 × 6in (25 × 15cm)	3in (8cm)	3½ minutes
LAVENDER	4 stems	10 × 6in (25 × 15cm)	3in (8cm)	3½ minutes
MARIGOLD	5 marigolds 10 marigolds	4 × 4in (10 × 10cm) 10 × 6in (25 × 15cm)	3in (8cm) 3in (8cm)	3 minutes 6 minutes
PANSY *(VIOLA TRICOLOR)*	8 pansies	10 × 6in (25 × 15cm)	2in (5cm)	2½ minutes
PRIMROSE	1 large cluster	4 × 4in (10 × 10cm)	4in (10cm)	4 minutes

*air dry by hanging if lanterns are to remain closed

PLANT	QUANTITY	BOX SIZE	AMOUNT OF SILICA GEL	TIME
RHODANTHE	4 stems	10 × 6in (25 × 15cm)	3in (8cm)	3½ minutes
ROSE	6 roses (thin petals and not fully open)	10 × 6in (25 × 15cm)	4in (10cm)	5½ minutes
	1 rosebud	not recommended	not recommended	use "open" method
	3 miniature roses	4 × 4in (10 × 10cm)	3in (8cm)	3½ minutes
SEA LAVENDER	4 stems	10 × 6in (25 × 15cm)	3in (8cm)	3 minutes
STATICE	5 stems	4 × 4in (10 × 10cm)	4in (10cm)	3 minutes
ZINNIA	3 zinnias	10 × 6in (25 × 15cm)	3in (8cm)	4 minutes
	5 zinnias	10 × 6in (25 × 15cm)	3in (8cm)	5 minutes

Leaves and Grasses

Because leaves are flat, you can stack 2 to 3 layers of leaves and silica gel in a box.

PLANT	QUANTITY	BOX SIZE	AMOUNT OF SILICA GEL	TIME
Lightweight leaves such as: MAPLE ELM STRAWBERRY ROSE CHRYSANTHEMUM SAGE	1 layer 3 layers	10 × 6in (25 × 15cm) 10 × 6in (25 × 15cm)	1in (2.5cm) 3in (8cm)	3 minutes 7 minutes
Thicker leaves such as: CAMELLIA BAY LAUREL HOLLY	1 layer 3 layers	10 × 6in (25 × 15cm) 10 × 6in (25 × 15cm)	1in (2.5cm) 3in (8cm)	5½ minutes 11 minutes
Coiled spray of IVY	12-15 leaves	10 × 6in (25 × 15cm)	3in (8cm)	10 minutes
SILVER-DOLLAR EUCALYPTUS	2 stems	10 × 6in (25 × 15cm)	3in (8cm)	10 minutes
Wild grasses such as: OATS WHEAT BARLEY	4-6 stems	10 × 6in (25 × 15cm)	3in (8cm)	5 minutes
BAMBOO	1 layer 3 layers	10 × 6in (25 × 15cm) 10 × 6in (25 × 15cm)	1in (2.5cm) 4in (10cm)	3 minutes 5½ minutes

METHOD CHART FOR DRYING PLANT MATERIALS

The following table provides a guide to just some of the plant materials you can dry by the methods described earlier in this chapter. It is, of course, by no means a complete list of all the possibilities, which are endless.

MATERIAL	PART OF PLANT MATERIAL TO BE DRIED	METHOD
Acanthus	Flower	Air drying
Achillea (yarrow)	Flower	Air drying
Anemone	Flower	Desiccant
Astilbe (spiraea)	Flower	Air drying
Bell heather	Flower	Air drying
Bells-of-Ireland	Bracts	Air drying and glycerine
Broom	Short flower sprays	Desiccant
Bulrush	Seedhead	Air drying
Buttercup	Flower	Desiccant
Camellia	Flower	Desiccant
Campion (Lychnis coronaria)	Flower	Air drying
Carnation	Flower	Desiccant
Celosia (cockscomb)	Flower	Air drying
Chamomile	Flower	Air drying
Chinese lantern	Seedhead	Air drying
Chive	Flower	Air drying
Chrysanthemum	Flower	Desiccant
Clarkia	Flower	Air drying
Clematis	Leaves and seedheads	Air drying
Copper beech	Leaves	Air drying and glycerine
Cornflower	Flower	Air drying and microwave
Corn-on-the-cob (corn)	Seedhead	Air drying
Daffodil	Flower	Desiccant
Dahlia	Flower	Desiccant
Daisy	Flower	Desiccant
Delphinium	Flower	Air drying and desiccant
Dock	Seedhead	Air drying
Dryandra	Flower	Air drying
Eryngium (sea holly)	Flower	Air drying

ABOVE *Fluffy spires of astilbe (spiraea) are most effectively dried by air drying.*

BELOW *Delicate cornflowers are suited to air or microwave drying.*

BELOW *Dahlia flower heads should be dried in desiccant and then stored in a box between tissue paper to preserve their shape.*

TOP & ABOVE *Small sprays of lilac and lily flowers can be successfully dried in desiccant.*

METHOD CHART FOR DRYING PLANT MATERIALS		
Fennel	Leaves	Microwave
Fescue grass	Seedhead	Air drying
Feverfew	Flower	Air drying and microwave
Forsythia	Short flower sprays	Desiccant
Giant hogweed	Seedhead	Air drying
Globe amaranth	Flower	Air drying
Golden rod	Flower	Air drying
Grape hyacinth	Flower Seedhead	Desiccant Air drying
Gypsophila (baby's breath)	Flower	Air drying
Helichrysum (strawflower)	Flower	Air drying
Holly	Leaves	Skeletonizing
Honesty	Seedhead	Air drying
Hop	Leaves and flowers	Air drying
Hydrangea	Bracts	Air drying
Ivy	Leaves	Skeletonizing
Jerusalem sage	Flower, leaves and seedhead	Air drying
Laburnum	Short flower sprays	Desiccant
Lady's mantle	Flower	Air drying and microwave
Larkspur	Flower	Air drying and desiccant
Laurel	Leaves	Skeletonizing
Lavatera (mallow)	Seedhead	Air drying
Lavender	Flower	Air drying
Lilac	Small flower sprays	Desiccant
Lily	Flower	Desiccant
Lily-of-the-valley	Flower	Desiccant
London pride	Flower	Desiccant
Love-in-a-mist	Flower and seedhead	Air drying
Love-lies-bleeding	Seedhead	Air drying
Lupin	Seedhead	Air drying
Magnolia	Flower Leaves	Desiccant Skeletonizing
Marjoram	Flower	Air drying and microwave
Millet	Seedhead	Air drying

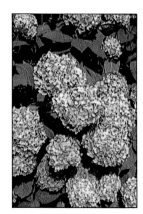

ABOVE *"Air dry" hydrangea bracts by standing them in a wide-necked container holding approximately 2in (5cm) of water.*

METHOD CHART FOR DRYING PLANT MATERIALS		
Mimosa	Flower	Air drying
Narcissus	Flower	Desiccant
Old-man's-beard	Leaves and seedhead	Air drying
Onion	Seedhead	Air drying
Pampas grass	Seedhead	Air drying
Pansy	Flower	Desiccant and microwave
Peony	Flower	Air drying and desiccant
Pine	Cone	Air drying
Pink	Flower	Air drying
Polyanthus	Flower	Desiccant
Poppy	Seedhead	Air drying
Pot marigold	Flower	Air drying and desiccant
Quaking grass	Seedhead	Air drying
Ranunculus	Flower	Desiccant
Rose	Bud, flower and leaves Fully opened flower	Air drying Desiccant
Rue	Seedhead	Air drying
Sage	Flower Leaves	Air drying Air drying and microwave
Sea lavender	Flower	Air drying
Sedge	Seedhead	Air drying
Senecio	Leaves	Air drying and microwave
Silver-leaved (white-leaf) everlasting	Flower	Air drying
Sorrel	Seedhead	Air drying
Statice	Flower	Air drying
Stock	Flower	Desiccant
Sunray (swan river) everlasting	Flower	Air drying
Sweet pea	Flower	Desiccant
Tansy	Flower	Air drying and microwave
Timothy grass	Seedhead	Air drying
Wallflower	Flower	Desiccant
Winged everlasting	Flower	Air drying
Zinnia	Flower	Desiccant

ABOVE *Once the flowers have died back, poppy seedheads can be air dried.*

ABOVE *Senecio leaves, air- or microwave-dried, will add subtle colour and texture to a design.*

CENTRE & ABOVE *Sweet peas and wallflowers should be dried in desiccant to preserve their delicate shapes.*

PRESERVING PLANTS

Many herb and spice leaves and some flowers can be successfully pressed for use in arrangements. Even leaves that are not obviously decorative in themselves – spearmint and lemon balm, for example – can provide a simple and effective backdrop for the more showy materials in an arrangement. Among the herbal flowers, nasturtium, chervil, dill and feverfew are all good subjects for pressing. And, like the methods for drying flowers, pressing is very straightforward and does not call for special equipment.

RIGHT *Large fleshy leaves such as fig and ivy can be preserved flat by completely immersing them in a glycerine and water solution.*

One of the main advantages of pressing leaves is that they can be picked for pressing at any time of year. This is the perfect way to capture the rosy hues of autumn leaves without having to resort to artificial dyes.

A more unusual way of preserving leaves is skeletonizing, in which the plant tissue breaks down and leaves only the veins and the outline of the leaf. These fragile structures can be wired together and used to give a delicate touch to an arrangement.

Foliage, bracts and berries preserved in glycerine take on a glossy, russet-tinted look that is perfect for adding autumnal cheer to your home in the depths of winter, or a bolder counterpart to brightly coloured flowers.

PRESSING
~

Pressing flowers and leaves, a hobby that takes many of us back to our childhood, is another way of drying and preserving plant material, one that leaves the subjects somewhat brittle and one-dimensional. Pressed flowers do not have much of a part to play in three-dimensional dried flower designs, but leaves can be useful. One advantage that pressing leaves has over preserving them in glycerine is that they can be captured at any time of year, not just when the sap is rising in the plant.

Effectively, this means that you can press fallen autumn leaves in all their glorious colours, from russet to gold, from scarlet to yellow, and use them to complement dried

LEFT & BELOW *Handle pressed flowers and leaves carefully. Like all other dried plant materials, they are brittle, and you should use tweezers or surgical tweezers to pick them up; a small paintbrush is useful for moving them around on a page. Store them in boxes or drawers away from strong light and, of course, in a dry room. Dried materials of all kinds are only too ready to re-absorb any moisture that comes their way.*

flowers in arrangements. The pressed leaves can be mounted on false wire stems and angled this way and that in designs, to give contrasting textural interest, visual weight at the base, and brilliant natural colour.

To press leaves you can use a standard flower press or you can use the traditional method of pressing leaves between sheets of absorbent paper in a heavy book. You can even press large leaves between sheets of newspaper placed under the carpet in a busy thoroughfare area of a room. Once dried, the leaves can be stored between tissues in a box, or kept in a book.

Whichever method you use, leave them in a dry place for several weeks; you may have to leave more substantial materials for up to six months. You will achieve greatly improved results by changing the blotting paper – which can be dried for re-use – two or three times at the beginning of the process.

It is a simple matter to mount pressed leaves on wire. According to the size and type of leaf, you can thread a stub wire in and out of the leaf along the central vein, or stick a wire along the centre of the leaf, using narrow florists' tape.

BELOW *Ethereal skeletonized holly leaves can be wired together for use in a dried flower decoration.*

SKELETONIZING
~

Skeletonized leaves, in which all the plant tissue has been eroded away, make delicate and attractive additions to a dried collection. You can sometimes find them beneath a magnolia or holly bush, a lacy shadow of their former selves, leaving just the vein structure of the leaf. Other leaves besides magnolia and holly that are suitable for skeletonizing include ivy and laurel.

To prepare skeletonized leaves by the traditional method involves leaving them in a pot of rainwater for weeks on end, a slimy process that will eventually break down the plant tissue and enable you to brush it away from the veins. A quicker and cleaner method is to boil the leaves in a cup of blue household detergent powder mixed with a pan of water for about 30 minutes. Wash the leaves under a cold tap and then, using an old toothbrush, brush away the broken-down tissue. Wash the skeletonized leaves again and, if you wish, immerse them in water with a little household bleach to freshen the colour. Blot the leaves between sheets of blotting paper until they are completely dry, and store them between tissues in a box.

PRESERVING IN GLYCERINE
~

Preserving foliage, bracts and berries in a glycerine solution greatly extends the range of long-lasting plant materials, offering you a collection of supple, glossy leaves which harmonize perfectly with the matt texture of dried flowers. All leaves change colour during the process, many of them taking on the deep russety-brown tints of autumn and a warm, copper-kettle kind of homely glow – just the look for arrangements you can enjoy throughout the winter.

Beech, one of the most popular leaves to preserve, turns a deep chestnut brown; laurel

RIGHT *Herbs and spices look attractive even during the preserving process. Stand the stems in a solution of glycerine and water and leave them until the leaves are supple and glossy. This selection includes the foliage of bay and rosemary, santolina and sage, and fennel and caraway in flower.*

turns such a dark brown that it is almost black; eucalyptus emerges from the process in a new deep gunmetal blue guise; and rosemary and bay turn deeper shades of green. Rose hips and berries shrink a little and some fade slightly. Red berries mellow to a deep orange, yellow berries (of holly, for example) turn deep golden orange, and blackberry fruits retain all the glorious depth of their colour.

The principle of the technique is simple, and one that cheats nature to a decorative advantage. The preserving solution is made up of one part glycerine to two parts very hot water. This is taken up by the stems and carried to every part of the plant material. As the water evaporates the glycerine is retained by the plant cells and preserves the material in its entirety. According to the size and type of the plant material, the process can take from a few days to several weeks.

The process is suitable for all deciduous and evergreen leaves, and for bracts such as bells-of-Ireland. The material must be gathered after the leaves are mature and while the sap is still rising in the plant, and so this places it as a summer pastime. You can store and re-use any left-over solution again, topping it up each time with the correct ratio of glycerine and water.

Inspect all foliage stems very carefully and snip off any damaged or discoloured leaves or bracts. Strip off the lower leaves and any that would be damaged by being trapped in the container. Scrape off the bark from woody stems for about 2in (5cm) from the base, and split or gently crush all of the stem ends so that they can more readily take up the solution.

Make up the solution, pour it into a lidded jar and shake it vigorously until it is thoroughly mixed. Pour it into containers (any type will do) to a depth of about 2in (5cm) and stand the stems in it, making sure that their ends are submerged.

Some large, fleshy leaves are best preserved by being totally immersed in the solution. These include aspidistra (cast-iron plant), fig and Japanese fatsia *(Fatsia japonica)*. Pour the solution into a shallow dish and immerse separate leaves.

Check the material every few days. Top up the containers with more of the solution if it has all been absorbed before preservation is complete. If the tips of the leaves start to dry out – and this can happen with some large specimens – rub them on both sides with cotton wool soaked in the solution. If beads of moisture appear on the surface, this is a sign that the plant material is already saturated with the solution, and should be removed straight away. The material is ready when the leaves or bracts have evenly changed colour and are completely supple. There should be no sign or sound of brittleness.

Once it is ready, remove the material from the solution. Dry stems thoroughly and wipe large leaves with cotton wool or a soft cloth to remove any stickiness. Dry immersed leaves thoroughly and "polish" them with a dry cloth. Store preserved leaves flat in boxes or upright in containers in a cool, dark room. The stems can safely be used in arrangements with both fresh and dried flowers, and will not absorb any further moisture.

RIGHT *Layers of spices and pot pourri can be used to conceal unattractive stems in a glass container.*

TIME CHART FOR PRESERVING FOLIAGE IN GLYCERINE		
The following table will give you some ideas of leaves to preserve, and the approximate time taken for the process.		
MATERIAL	**NOTES**	**APPROXIMATE NUMBER OF WEEKS TO PRESERVE**
Aspidistra (cast-iron plant)	Immerse in solution	2-3
Bay	Leaves deepen to dark green	2
Beech	Cut when fully mature. Preserve in large or small sprays	½-1
Bells-of-Ireland	Hang upside-down to dry after preserving	3
Berberis (barberry)	Preserve long stems. Leaves turn dark brown	3
Blackberry	Treat sprays of leaves complete with berries	3
Cotoneaster	Leaves turn leathery brown, silver on reverse	3-4
Cypress	Treat flat fan-shaped leaves complete with "cones"	3-4
Dock	Treat long spikes of seedheads, which turn a deeper shade of red	2
Escallonia	Treat long stems of the minute leaves. They make good outlines in designs	2
Eucalyptus	Leaves darken and retain their gunmetal appearance	2-3
Fig	Immerse single leaves	1-2
Hellebore	Leaves turn light brown	3
Holly	Treat sprays of leaves and berries. Spray berries with hair lacquer	3
Ivy	Immerse very large leaves. Treat stems complete with berries	1½-2 3
Japanese fatsia (Fatsia japonica)	Immerse in solution. Leaves turn leathery brown	2-3
Laurel	Leaves turn almost black	4
Mahonia	Leaves sometimes give two-tone effect	3-5
Maidenhair fern	Can preserve leaves at any time of year	2
Maple	Treat single leaves and clusters of keys	2
Mistletoe	Treat small sprays with berries	2
Oak	Oak-apples and acorns can be preserved on the stems	2-3
Old-man's-beard	Gather before flowers open. Spray with hair lacquer after preserving	2

ABOVE *Berberis (barberry) leaves will turn dark brown during the preserving process.*

ABOVE *Sprays of holly – together with their berries – can be preserved in glycerine. Red berries take on a rich orange hue.*

ABOVE *Once preserved, long stems of escallonia with their minute leaves can be used to make effective outlines in a design.*

BELOW *Preserve sprays of rhododendron when the flowers are in bud.*

TIME CHART FOR PRESERVING FOLIAGE IN GLYCERINE		
MATERIAL	NOTES	APPROXIMATE NUMBER OF WEEKS TO PRESERVE
Peony	Leaves turn dark olive green with light contrasting veins	2
Pyracantha	Treat sprays with berries	3
Raspberry	Leaves turn dark red with silver undersides	2
Rhododendron	Preserve leaf sprays with young, tight buds	3
Rose	Young shoots of wild roses preserve well. Boil solution to preserve	2
Rose hips	Spray hips with hair lacquer after preserving	2-3
Rosemary	Leaves retain their scent	2
Rowan (mountain ash)	Preserve sprays of leaves and berries. Leaves turn nut brown	2
Silver birch	Use solution at boiling point	4
Sweet (Spanish) chestnut	Preserve some with catkins	1½-2
Sycamore	Treat leaves and keys	1-1½
Viburnum	Leaves turn deep brown with olive green on reverse	3
Yew	Leaves can be preserved at any time. Berries are not reliable in the preserving process; they often wither	3

ABOVE *Viburnum leaves will turn dark brown with olive green on the reverse when preserved in glycerine.*

LEFT *Pyracantha berries and rose hips, fern leaves and bells-of-Ireland bracts can all be preserved in a glycerine and water solution.*

Methods and Materials

From a luxuriant circlet of midsummer flowers to a hoop of sun-bleached oats; from a ribbon of trailing leaves and fresh or dried flowers edging a celebration table to a centrepiece of jewel-like blooms on a formal dining table – the elegance and style of floral decorations depends on the base on which each is made.

Of course, you need not use any supporting materials (foam, wire or adhesives) at all. But by using these supports, you can create a greater range of designs than you might have thought possible.

The tools of flowercraft work best when they are completely unobtrusive. Just as a magician must keep wires, strings and hidden pockets completely secret from the audience, so the flower arranger must create as natural a look as possible by making sure that all means of support are completely hidden. This is easily done by using an abundance of plant material to camouflage any artificial means of support, or by using marble chippings or glass beads to conceal wired stems.

The right container can turn a simple floral arrangement into an outstanding design feature. Don't limit yourself to vases as flower containers: tumblers, jugs, baskets and bowls work just as well. If you are using dried flowers, your container need not even be waterproof.

A bunch of gypsophila (baby's breath) in a wine jug making a natural "lace curtain" in a cottage window; a blue and white jug of statice in a sunny breakfast corner; a silver vase of dainty pink rosebuds on a dressing table – it is possible to compose pretty arrangements of flowers with no special equipment at all. However, by using a selection of stem-holding materials, wires and tapes – equipment which is known as mechanics – it is possible to greatly extend the range of containers you can use and thus the designs you can achieve. It would, for example, be very difficult to arrange a glorious basket of peonies, lavender, marjoram and globe thistle for a summer fireplace with no hidden support for the stems. Dried flower stems are brittle and wayward, and when massed together have a habit of thrusting upwards and outwards if they are not tamed in some way.

Stem-holding Materials
~

New enthusiasts to the art of decorating with dried flowers may shy away from using stem-holding materials, thinking that they add a complication and make natural-looking designs more difficult to achieve. In fact, the reverse is true. By using some kind of support for the stems, the element of chance is eliminated, and the arranger can concentrate more fully on the design he or she wishes to create.

There are two types of florists' foam: the absorbent type is for use with fresh flowers and foliage.

The principal stem-holding material made specially for use with dried flowers is dry foam. This foam may be brown or grey, is as light as a feather and has a slightly sparkly surface. It must be emphasized that its fresh-

RIGHT *A selection of the bases, rings and wreaths that you are able to buy or make. From top left, clockwise: twisted grass stem wreath, corn dolly wreath, absorbent foam ring, twisted-twig rings, and the same ring spray-painted.*

flower counterpart, absorbent foam (which is usually green), should not be used in its unsoaked state for dried flower arrangements, since it does not give the necessary degree of grip and is, besides, liable to break up. Both types are available in a block a little larger than a household brick, in small cylinders, and in spheres, cones and rings of various sizes.

The foam blocks may be used in their entirety for large designs; indeed two or more bricks may be needed for arrangements on large pedestals or in wide baskets. You can also think of the blocks as a designer-friendly raw material you can cut to any size and shape, to fit or fill any type of container and help you to achieve any design you have in mind. All you need is a sharp knife to cut the foam and a sheet of newspaper to cover your working surface and catch the shiny dust that comes away when the foam is cut.

The cylinders, about 2¼in (5.5cm) deep and 3in (8cm) across, may be used alone, wedged into the neck of a container such as a teapot or coffee pot, for example, or used in conjunction with plastic saucers specially made for the purpose, with a ridged indentation that exactly matches the diameter of the foam.

The spheres may be used to create designs such as a dried flower hanging ball. A pretty example would be a ball composed of delicate grasses and, for a countryside look, deep blue cornflowers to hang in a window or an alcove. Foam spheres are also used to create indoor trees, the small and medium sizes for tabletop designs and the large size for a floor-standing model.

The cones are used for pyramid designs and may be used alone, when placed on a dish or board, or to create a stylized "topiary" tree, when the shape is mounted on a twig or cane and set realistically in a flower pot or other container (see page 106).

Foam rings are used to create wall or table-top designs, circlets of flowers and seedheads to grace any room from the bedroom to the kitchen. Designs of this kind are described fully on pages 77 to 101.

The other principal stem-holding material is 2in- (5cm)-wide wire-mesh netting, which you can buy by the yard or the metre from garden-supply shops, where it is also known as chicken wire. Florists and some floral art clubs sell a more refined version in which the netting is coated with green plastic. To use the netting you crush it into a mound or ball and wedge it to fill the neck of a container. This may be an urn, a wide-necked vase, a deep bowl or a basket. As the wire is scrunched up it forms an entangled mass with uneven but smaller-than-original holes – just what is needed to anchor and angle dried flower stems.

Florists' setting clay, sold packaged in lumps of various weights, can be used as a stem holder, although that is not its main purpose. The green clay may be used on, for example, a woven placemat if you want to create a flower spray on the textured background. A small lump of the clay pressed on to the surface will hold the stems firmly – and permanently, since it soon sets as hard as cement.

Another use for setting clay is to anchor the "trunk" element of designer table-top trees into their pots. Larger trees are usually set in plaster of Paris, a cheaper material more suited to the quantity needed for floor-standing designs.

Pinholders may be used with dried as well as fresh flowers. These heavy weights with vertical spikes are available in various shapes and are especially useful for designs built up on a flat surface such as a board or tray. Stems can be pressed between the spikes to stand upright or to angle this way and that. Large preserved or pressed leaves can be included in the base of the design to conceal the holder, or it may be masked by a handful of gravel or marble chippings.

FIXING MATERIALS
~

Adhesive clay (not to be confused with setting clay) is an extra-tacky clay which is used to secure, for example, a plastic foam-holding saucer to the neck of a container. You may decide to turn a glass wine carafe into a pedestal by fitting it with a saucer of foam. A few dabs of adhesive clay around the rim secures the saucer in place.

The clay is also used to fix plastic spikes to a container. These four-pronged spikes can be used to hold foam in place. First press a dab or two of the clay on to the base of the spike. Press it in place in the container and then press on the foam. The clay is sold in strips, on a reel or in cut lengths. It is dark green, about $\frac{1}{2}$in (1cm) wide and sold with a paper backing. The surfaces it is used on must be completely dry, but once it is in place it will not be dislodged by subsequent moisture.

Florists' adhesive tape, which is sticky on one side and sticks well to non-porous and shiny surfaces, is useful to fix foam firmly into containers. Used from side to side, up and over the foam and down on to the container, it does a belt-and-braces job of reinforcing any other means of securing the foam. It is not usually necessary to take this extra precaution with small designs but it is a worthwhile insurance when large containers are used. The tape can also be used in addition to adhesive clay to fix plastic foam-holders to other containers.

WIRING
~

Many of the mechanics used with dried flowers will be familiar to anyone used to designing with fresh flowers, since the method of preparing the containers is similar. One technique which applies more specifically to dried flower designs is wiring: wiring flower heads on to false stems; wiring short natural stems on to longer wire ones; extending natural hollow stems by inserting a wire; wiring bunches of small-scale materials together to make a massed effect (for example, snippings of golden rod) and wiring dried cones, nuts and other materials to decorate swags and ribbons. In short, the technique of wiring has an important part to play in dried flower design, and is one that should be practised until it can be achieved quickly, easily and above all neatly.

We saw earlier that some flowers, helichrysums (strawflowers) especially, are apt to part company with their natural stems and need to be given false ones, in this case a medium-gauge stub wire. Stub wires are available in several thicknesses, from fine through medium to heavy gauge, and in lengths from 3½ to 18in (9 to 45.5cm). Usually two or three types of stub wire will be sufficient; there is certainly no need to invest in the whole range!

Fine silver binding wire, very similar to fuse wire, is used to bind stub wires to short lengths of natural stem when, for example,

flowers have been dried in desiccants. This wire is sold in rolls and is sometimes known as rose wire. A good tip when using it is to place the roll in a cup so that it does not roll off the table or get tangled. A heavier-gauge reel wire, which may be black or brown, is useful when wiring dried materials to swags and rings.

Lengths of split cane, sold in bundles by some florists, are used to provide or lengthen stems of heavy-headed flowers such as chrysanthemums and pom-pom dahlias – any flowers, in fact, which would be top-heavy if they were mounted on a wire. If such flowers have no natural stem at all, it will be necessary to mount them on a heavy-gauge stub wire, pushing it up from the base of the flower, bending over a short hook and pulling that through into the flower centre. The length of wire extending beneath the flower can then be bound on to a cane, using fine roll wire.

Cones have many decorative uses in dried flower designs, and are especially appreciated in winter arrangements and those made for Christmas. To wire cones and give them a

LEFT *These are some of the materials used in the composition of the arrangements featured in the book.*
1 *nasturtiums*
2 *thick cord*
3 *string*
4 *twine*
5 *clear all-purpose glue*
6 *microwave-dried cornflowers*
7 *heavy-gauge wire*
8 *roll of fine silver wire*
9 *medium-gauge stub wires*
10 *fine silver wires*
11 *florists' scissors*
12 *wire cutters*

false stem use a heavy or medium-gauge stub wire, according to the size of cone. Wrap one end of the wire inside and around the lowest row of scales leaving 2in (5cm) of the wire jutting out. Twist the two ends together tightly and bend them to form a straight stem beneath the cone. If the cone is to be inserted into a foam shape such as a ring, this stem length should be sufficient. If it is to be used in an arrangement it will be necessary to wire on a full-length false stem. Place a split cane or heavy-gauge stub wire against the short stem and bind them together with silver roll wire.

PREPARING CONTAINERS
~

The degree of care taken in preparing containers pays dividends in the finished design. When some kind of holding material is needed, as it is with shallow, wide-necked or large containers, the first question is whether to use dry foam or crumpled wire-mesh netting. In general, foam is preferred for shallow containers such as bowls and dishes and chicken wire for deep ones such as fish-bowl-shaped vases and most baskets.

To shape foam to fit the base of a shallow bowl, press the bowl on to a block of foam to make an indent, then cut around it. Using a sharp knife, sculpt the foam to come to a dome shape in the centre, with an even, gentle curve sloping down at the sides. Press a plastic spike the base of the container with adhesive clay and push the foam on to the prongs.

If you want to angle some stems horizontally in the design, or have them slanting downwards over the rim of the container, shape the foam to extend about 2in (5cm) above the rim. This extra height will then enable you to position stems at any angle.

Glass containers pose a special problem, because dried flower stems and taped artificial ones do not look well when massed in the base of a container. If you are using a tall glass vase or wine carafe you can turn it into a simulated pedestal by fitting a foam-holding saucer and a cylinder of dry foam to the top in the way described earlier. The stems will all be held high above the container, and the holding material concealed behind flowers and leaves pressed close against the foam.

If you use a wide-necked glass trough, you can tackle the situation in a completely different way by concealing a block of foam inside it. Cut the foam to almost fill the rectangular container, but leave a cavity on all four sides. Firmly fix the foam in place on a plastic prong, then fill the gap between the dry foam and the glass walls with a decorative natural material. This could be pot pourri, dry sphagnum moss or lichen moss.

There is nothing difficult about using crumpled wire in the neck of a container. Take a piece of wire in both hands, tuck in the exposed ends and crush it into a ball to fit the neck of a container. Secure the wire to the container in whatever way is appropriate. You can wire it to the handles of a basket, using stub wires or roll wire, or fix it to a ceramic container by criss-crossing adhesive tape over the wire netting and down on to the container. For most designs it is best to shape the wire into a dome which curves gently into a mound above the rim of the container. This will enable you to position stems at a rakish angle.

Whenever you use a stem-holding material of any kind it is important to conceal it. Recessing flowers and leaves into the heart of the design and having some materials on very short stems is one way of ensuring concealment. Another way is to cover the foam with a layer of sphagnum moss anchored in place with bent stub wires used as staples. If traces of the natural moss are visible in the finished design all is not lost.

Moss can be used in other decorative ways, too. You can convert the most utilitarian household container – anything from a plastic ice-cream tub to a shoe box – by covering it with a thick layer of dry sphagnum moss,

RIGHT *The basic tools of flower arranging include florist's foam in various shapes, a block of dry florist's foam or some chicken wire, florist's tape, medium-gauge floral wire, fine gauge floral wire, and florist's scissors.*

hay, or a mixture including some dried flowers. Paint the surface of the container with clear, quick-setting glue and press on handfuls of moss or hay. Add more of the mixture until the surface is completely covered then, tie the container around with two or three bands of plaited raffia.

The natural colours of baskets are particularly complementary to flowers. But there may be times when you feel that a design would benefit from a closer colour link between the container and its contents. Painted baskets make equally attractive containers and can be colour-matched to the plant materials. If you have an open-weave basket or one that needs a face-lift you can decorate it with dried stems of lavender or thyme, weaving or sticking them all over the basket, around the rim or over the handle. Lavender baskets made in this way are expensive to buy.

Baskets take well to bands of colour, such as vertical, horizontal or diagonal stripes of, say, heathery blue and crushed strawberry pink. Old ceramic vases, discarded teapots, coffee mugs and many other household items can be brought into decorative service with a splash of paint. And for one technique, spatter-painting, splash is the word. Paint the container with one colour and allow it to dry, then spatter it with short bursts of a second colour. Ragwork is another technique which looks well on ceramic or other containers. Paint the surface with colour and dab it with a small piece of plastic sponge to give it a textured effect.

Gradually, as you build up a collection of dried materials, holding material and other aids, and a variety of containers, you will have all it takes to create a multitude of designs for your home and for special occasions.

A Sense of Design

Begin to use flowers in your home by remembering that rules are made to be broken. The guidelines to design given in this chapter are a starting point to thinking about mixing colours, choosing shapes, and finding balance. As you gain confidence in your creativity and your artist's eye, you will be able to bend and break the rules and still come up with striking arrangements that work beautifully.

Backgrounds have such an important influence on the overall effect of a floral design that they should be thought through at the very earliest planning stages. The same flower arrangement may be a real eye-catcher against a contrasting background, or have an understated look in a complementary setting. Size and scale, too, need to be considered: flowers may be lost in too large an area, or look out of proportion in a smaller space. Above all, be guided by the style of the flowers themselves: match sleek lilies with a minimalist decor, or a busy froth of gypsophila (baby's breath) with a more relaxed setting.

If you keep a stock of dried and preserved plant materials to hand, you will be able to individualize store-bought bouquets to suit a particular spot in your home. Non-floral ingredients, particularly, will give you enormous scope to adapt arrangements to suit their setting: pine cones, bundles of cinnamon sticks, paper or raffia bows, artificial clusters of berries – a few of these kept to hand make the possibilities limitless.

Larkspur and lavender, helichrysums (strawflowers) and statice, exciting colours and exotic seedheads – florists and department stores have an ever-increasing display of dried flowers and other plant materials. While you are gradually building up your collection of your own dried and preserved flowers and leaves, you can supplement it with commercially dried – and often dyed – materials in an inspiring range of colours.

Dyed seedheads and grasses can greatly extend the colour span of your collection but be sure, before you buy them, that they will harmonize with your existing stock. Some of the more vibrant colours do not look at all natural, and can dominate any group. Hold bunches of flowers and grasses in your hand, half-close your eyes and assess the effect of the tapestry of colour. If one bunch seems to strike a jarring note, exchange it for another until you have a selection you like.

Enhance your collection, too, with unusual and exotic materials from overseas. Lotus flower seedheads, their trumpet shapes full of holes; lufa seedpods with their chestnut-brown colouring and ridged texture; plumosum heads with their untidy spiky appearance; protea flowers in various stages of development; jhuta, their open pods like carved wooden flowers – these materials in neutral shades and warm rich browns blend well with home-spun seedheads, with cones and nuts, and with spices like cinnamon quills and nutmeg. Buying these "exotics", as florists call them, need not break the bank. You can buy them gradually, a few at a time, confident that with careful handling they will last indefinitely, a once-in-a-lifetime investment.

SIZING UP
THE BACKGROUND
~

Before creating a flower arrangement, consider carefully the background against which it will be seen. Dried flower designs in particular take a little time and patience to compose and will give you pleasure for many months to come, so it is important that they are at one with their surroundings.

Look at each room critically and consider whether a lasting flower arrangement should provide a highlight of colour or should blend in with the furnishings. If a room is furnished in neutral shades of cream and brown it may be that a design in tones of, say, orange and yellow or blue and purple may be just what it needs to bring the scheme to life. A basket of golden statice bunches in the hearth or a blue and white jug of purple statice on a table would become the focal point of the room, a sharp, attention-seeking accent of colour.

There may be a secondary colour in the room which could be accentuated in your choice of flowers. Perhaps the curtains or wallpaper have a hint of pale pink that gives a cue for a floral design in the same hue. A deeper or brighter shade of pink picked up in the flowers would create a pleasant harmony. It may be that a country-style blend of cream and pink helichrysums (strawflowers) and larkspur, pink gypsophila (baby's breath) and brighter pink sunray (swan river) everlastings would look tailor-made for the room. Or perhaps a mass of flowers of a single type – bunches of helichrysums (strawflowers) in varying shades of pink – would create a more eye-catching display.

If the room – a hall, perhaps – is furnished in black, white and grey, an elegant and uncompromising scheme, flowers in a primary colour may be needed to hold the attention. Pinks and pale blues, soft yellows and mauves would all look faded and bleached against the stark contrast of the surroundings. Go for flowers in bright red, sunshine yellow or strident blue. You could choose a jug of brilliant red peonies, their colour commanding attention from every angle, or a bowl of deep red roses to strike a slightly softer note. You could arrange statice in the sharpest tones of yellow with pure white gypsophila (baby's breath) or lacy sea lavender for a slightly veiled effect or, more simply, place a pot of yellow tansy where it will make the strongest impression. In the blue theme, you could arrange a tall white jug of blue and white larkspur or a bright blue jug of pure white dried flowers, a blend of different shapes, sizes and textures that would harmonize perfectly with the room

LEFT *A striking wall arrangement, this horizontal spray uses hydrangea, cornflowers, rosebuds, helichrysums (strawflowers) and sea lavender. It would add a beautiful flourish above a wall mirror, a fireplace or a doorway.*

scheme. The use of colour and the relationship of one colour to another is explained more fully in the colour wheel panel on page 51.

Important as colour is in creating harmonious effects, it is not the only consideration when planning a significant flower arrangement for a room. The size and scale of any patterned furnishings has to be taken into account when choosing the flowers, the container and the style of the design. Depending on the complexity or otherwise of the furnishings, a flower arrangement may blend so discreetly with the background as to be almost unnoticeable, or it may stand out boldly, becoming the focal point of the room.

If the walls and curtains are plain or textured, there are no limitations on the designs you can create to display there. A basket of dried flowers arranged singly will have all the charm of a mixed herbaceous border in summer, and every flower will be seen.

If the background against which the arrangement is seen has a bold or busy pattern, the same basket may look fussy and cluttered, and not at all at home in its environment. In these circumstances it is better to compose an arrangement in a limited colour range, or one using large blocks of colour that will show up well against the pattern.

Designs in a single colour blended with cream or white or a range of tints from, say, palest pink to richest red put emphasis on the shape and texture of the flowers, and present an interesting challenge to the flower arranger.

If the background pattern of walls or curtains is small – it may be composed of small posies of flowers or a tracery of flowers and foliage – a flower display using well-defined blocks of colour would be more effective than one in which the materials are arranged singly. To achieve this effect you simply arrange the materials in bunches or clusters: not one pencil-slim side shoot of fluffy golden rod but several, wired together to form a sunshine yellow mass of colour; not one single pinky-peach helichrysum (strawflower) creating a small pool of colour, but five or six, wired together and creating a real splash; not single feverfew flowers inserting snow-white polka dots among their more colourful neighbours, but ten or fifteen bunched together to form sizeable highlights which could become a focal point of the design. When dried materials are arranged in this way the design has a far more pronounced colour impact and will be able to hold its own against even a multi-patterned background.

Another way to maximize the colour impact is to arrange flowers in blocks of colour. You might have a deep earthenware bowl and a medley of flowers in pink, blue, gold and cream. Instead of composing the arrangement so that the colours are evenly distributed throughout the design, try arranging them in rainbow blocks, all the pink ones in one quarter, all the blue ones in another, and so on. The visual effect is exciting, and very unusual. As a variation on this theme, you can arrange flowers in stripes according to their colour. You might have a rectangular basket fitted with a piece of crumpled wire-mesh netting and an armful of flowers in blue, white and yellow. Divide the flowers into their separate colours and arrange them blue, white, yellow, white across the basket for a modern look and a design that will stand up to the fiercest competition from furnishing patterns.

A dining table is an easy background for flower arrangements. Seen against the plain wood background even the smallest and most intricate designs show up well. Consider the colour tone of the wood and plan pastel and bright colours to contrast with a dark surface, or deeper tones to be silhouetted against pale wood. If you cover the table with a patterned cloth, even a heavy lace one, take this into consideration when planning the flower arrangements. All the rules about a bolder approach and using stronger colour blocks will apply.

RIGHT Arranging flowers to suit a certain area with a specific background can be a challenge. Here the colours of the plants used – lavender, golden rod and fresh chillies are almost mirrored by the blues, yellows and greens of this wallpaper.

FLOWER SHAPES

There are three basic shapes among the whole beautiful range of flowers and, in a mixed display, it is effective to include them all.

• First and foremost, and by far the largest group, are the full, round flowers such as helichrysums (strawflowers), roses, peonies and mop-headed hydrangeas and, among the seedheads, onion, poppy, globe thistle and carline thistle. These are the shapes to arrange at the heart of a design and close to the centre base, where they will become the focal point.

• Next there are the sprays, of statice, lavender, larkspur and astilbe (spiraea), dock, love-lies-bleeding and many others. These materials, with their straight stems and spiky characteristics, are the ones to define the height and width of a design, to draw the outlines and feature in the extremities.

• And then there are the flowers and grasses with lacy shapes that give a soft, veiled effect to an arrangement and blur harsher outlines. These include sea lavender, gypsophila (baby's breath) and lady's mantle, miniature everlasting *(Pithocarpa corymbulosa)*, seacrest *(Helichrysum cordatum)*, pampas and other grasses.

• A design which draws freely from these three groups will have heightened interest, and be rich in texture. When the flowers and seedheads are in a limited colour range, the accent on the texture is strengthened and the contrasting shapes appear more pronounced.

LEFT *Even before they are arranged, these microwave-dried flowers make a delightful composition with their clear, bright colours and variety of textures. Those in the basket include peonies, sea lavender, quaking grass, love-in-a-mist, larkspur, rosebuds, helichrysums (strawflowers), statice and lady's mantle.*

ADDED COLOUR

~

With every colour in the rainbow represented in the whole wonderful world of fresh and dried flowers, it is reasonable to take the view that you cannot improve on nature. But there are instances when the addition of nearly natural or sheer fun colours can extend your range of plant materials in an interesting and enlivening way. Take seedheads, for example. Most of them have varied and fascinating shapes, yet few of them make a generous contribution to a design in colour terms. Sometimes the neutral tones of creamy-beige poppyheads, say, can be a welcome foil to other, more colourful materials such as jewel-bright dried peonies. But there are occasions (Christmas is one) when those seedheads would be the perfect design accessory, if only they were red.

Take sea lavender, a plant that dries into multi-flowered spikes which are virtually everlasting and immensely versatile, but not very colourful. Snippings of the stems, in all their wayward directions, add pretty, ragged outlines to a dried flower wreath, give a dainty summery look to a dried flower garland, and contrast effectively with round and spherical flowers of all kinds. If your stock of sea lavender is uniformly pearly-white, as much of it is, buy a specialist non-toxic flower spray-paint, spread out the dried plant on ample sheets of newspaper and colour it pink, blue, yellow or the shade of your choice.

And, just for fun, take honesty, an invaluable plant for bringing a dash of natural glint and glitter to Christmas and party decorations. Add a few sprays of the silvery discs to brighten evergreen wreaths and garlands; make a bright-as-a-beacon wreath of tightly

THE COLOUR WHEEL

If you have ever wondered why blue and orange flowers make such a perfect partnership, each bloom bringing out the best in its neighbour, or why red flowers look at their most vibrant when arranged with green foliage, the answer is to be found in the colour wheel. This is an arrangement of colours, in the order in which they appear in the rainbow, which enables you to tell at a glance which colours are complementary and which ones are harmonious.

● To make a colour wheel, draw circles and divide them into six equal segments. Colour or write in the three primary colours – blue, yellow and red – in three alternate spaces around the outer wheel. Primary colours are the ones that cannot be made by mixing other colours together. (See Wheel 1.)

● Between the primary colours are the secondary ones, made by mixing together the colours on either side. This places green between blue and yellow, orange between yellow and red and mauve between red and blue. (See Wheel 1.)

● The most complementary colours are the ones facing each other on the wheel: the attraction of opposites – blue cornflowers and orange lilies, or blue flowers seen against an orange background; yellow daffodils and mauve irises; red roses and green nicotiana, or red flowers placed against a green wall. These are the combinations to go for to achieve the most eye-catching and strident effects. (See Wheel 2.)

● Harmonious colours, ones which blend well together for a more subtle effect, are those next to each other on the wheel: blue and green, or yellow, orange and red (see Wheel 3). Create a design in these colour combinations and no single flower or flower colour will stand out, or be seen to such full effect.

WHEEL 1:
PRIMARY AND SECONDARY COLOURS;

WHEEL 2:
COMPLEMENTARY COLOURS

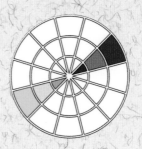

WHEEL 3:
HARMONIOUS COLOURS

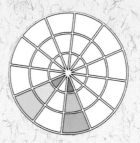

TINTS AND TONES

● Colours also have the ability to deceive the eye – a useful ploy in flower arranging. "Cool" colours such as blue and green seem further away, while "warm" colours such as red and orange seem closer than they are. Experiment for yourself when you are next composing a multi-coloured arrangement. Recess blue and green materials in the heart of the design and have the reds and oranges thrusting forwards. The effect will be to exaggerate the reality and give the design an enhanced dimension.

● Each of the six colours has a wide range of variables: not only the basic hue but all the tints, tones and shades that are so apparent in any selection of flowers. A tint is the basic hue mixed with white (see the middle band of Wheel 1). A tone is the basic colour mixed with grey (see inner band of Wheel 1), and a shade is the basic hue blended with black. For the most subtle and agreeable effects, you can arrange flowers in a single colour, but in several tints, tones and shades of that colour – a cluster of helichrysums (strawflowers) for example, from palest pink through the middle tones to deepest red, or a bowl of mauve pansies and chive flowers with purple marjoram set against a pale mauve background.

packed honesty sprays alone, or add a few snippings to catch the light in designs composed of matt-surfaced flowers. But there is no need to leave it there. Retain the natural gloss but add a nearly neutral colour, such as pale green or pale pink, by spatter-spraying the seed discs. It's honesty with a most attractive difference.

LEAF COLOUR
~

The technique of preserving leaves in a glycerine solution (see pages 35 to 39) has a natural colouring effect, darkening the tissues until laurel leaves emerge nearly black, eucalyptus turns deep gunmetal blue, rosemary and bay take on an even deeper shade of green, and beech becomes dark chestnut brown. Since the range of colour in preserved mat-

erials is somewhat limited it is interesting to experiment by adding a little commercial dye to the glycerine solution. In this way the plant material takes up, not only the preserving agent, but colour, too, and it is possible to obtain some fascinating effects. Try adding green dye when preserving beech, oak, maple and chestnut leaves, ivy, rhododendron, choisya and ferns. The depth and brightness of the resultant colour makes the leaves a pleasing choice for natural-looking and long-lasting garlands, and an interesting alternative to the use of familiar evergreens.

For more "authentic" autumnal tints, you can add red dye to the preserving solution for eucalyptus leaves, which become copper-bronze, and to copper beech, which takes on a cheerful fieriness. Lime bracts, which make useful components in long-lasting wreaths, take well to a rust-coloured dye.

LEFT *This delightful basket arrangement of peonies, rosebuds, helichrysums (strawflowers) and sea lavender cleverly conceals the vital mechanics – crumpled chicken wire held firmly in place with strips of adhesive tape.*

CHOOSING CONTAINERS

~

When it comes to choosing containers for dried and preserved materials, it is a case of anything goes. A container does not need to be waterproof, does not need to contain an inner water-holding vessel, and does not even need to have an aperture. You can fix a saucer of foam to a tall candlestick and use it as a simulated pedestal, or fix dried flowers to a one-dimensional background such as a woven placemat or a flat hanging-basket shape to create a lively wall-hanging.

BASKETS

Baskets of all kinds have a special affinity with dried flowers and are likely to feature prominently in any enthusiast's collection of containers. Large, deep baskets to hold a vibrant display of dried flowers in a fireplace; round, deep shopping baskets to stand in a room corner; circular willow baskets to decorate a dining table; they all look tailor-made for dried flower displays.

Before making your choice of basket for any given situation, consider its size carefully. If you are planning a fan-shaped arrangement with long spires of larkspur and clarkia angled away at each side, the finished design could be anything up to twice the width of the container. And it could be expensive in its use of dried materials.

One of the secrets of successful flower arranging is that the container should be packed with flowers, to give a look of luxury. It is far more effective to have a smaller container filled to overflowing with a generous display of dried materials than a larger one that looks sparse and unfinished. Not only that, when flowers are arranged to give a filled-in tapestry effect, the stems, be they wire, cane or natural, are completely hidden from view by the massed flowerheads. This is the look of a well-stocked garden in high summer, and is the effect to aim for in all dried flower designs.

You might have a large, flat basket with a looped handle or two side handles. One way to arrange it, using foam as the holding material, would be to position dried flower stems vertically: straight, soldierly stems of, say, wheat, lavender, roses and love-in-a-mist as erect as when they are growing. Another way, which heightens the interest, is to arrange several separate containers to stand in the basket. You might have a collection of small posy baskets, the kind you can buy cheaply at charity shops, a collection of pottery beakers, or several earthenware pots. Arrange each container with its own limited colour range of materials – cream and white in one, blue and cream in another – and stand the containers side by side in the basket. Displayed on a hall table, a chest of drawers or a sideboard, the basket would be full of interest and could become – as you rearrange the separate containers – a constantly changing display.

Small posy baskets make perfect individual containers for a dining table, arrangements that can be at the ready to decorate the most impromptu of lunch or dinner parties. Fill the aperture with crumpled wire-mesh netting and arrange nosegays of small dried flowers, side shoots and clippings. Small-scale materials of this kind may be left over from a large display in the room, and would in that case make a perfect match.

Baskets are as versatile as they are decorative. You can buy designs specially made to hang on the wall, with a flat back and a curved, pouched front to take a drooping, trailing, overhanging display of dried materials. Consider arranging a wall basket in rich autumnal tones of brown and gold, with trails of preserved hops and copper beech leaves, sprays of dried oak foliage, teasels, hogweed seedheads and brilliant clusters of tansy and golden rod. Or take a completely different approach and fill a rugged basket with a more delicate selection of pinks and blues, with preserved leaves and old-man's-beard to form a colour link. Hang a basket between two doors or windows, above a piece of furniture, on a .door or on a little-used cupboard – many places are ideal.

Narrow shoulder baskets make perfect wall-hangings, too. Fill one side of a basket with a diagonally placed sheaf of dried wheat, barley or oats, with an armful of dried grasses, or with bunches of dried statice, for a made-in-moments display that is every bit as eye-catching as an intricate arrangement. Or fill the aperture with a block or two of dried foam and create a fan shape of dried materials to hang over a chimney-piece or stand in the hearth.

Coloured baskets have a separate role to play. They can be colour-matched to any soft furnishings or decorating scheme, but seem especially appropriate in a bedroom. A basket sprayed in deep purple looks effective with pale pink peonies, purple marjoram and lavender, and could fill a room corner or stand on a chest of drawers. A painted posy basket filled with rosebuds would be pretty on a dressing-table, and a shoulder bag woven in coloured stripes could be filled with trailing flowers and hung on a bed post or door.

If you think that natural willow and other woven baskets are too rugged for your home, consider prettying them up in a number of ways. You can thread satin or lace ribbon through the upright spokes and finish it with a flourish, a generous bow with trailing ends, or bind the handle round and round with ribbon. You can line the edge of a basket with lacy white or gold doilies, the decorative edging overlapping the rim. And you can finish off a dried flower design with a sizeable bow of "raffia" paper ribbon, chosen to match one of the prominent flower colours.

METAL CONTAINERS

The glint and gleam of metal adds a sparkle to dried materials that are, in the main, matt and lacking in sheen. A copper milk jug brimming over with a winter mixture of preserved leaves, golden rod, yellow achillea (yarrow), Chinese lanterns and fir cones; a pewter sugar bowl pretty as a picture with pink sunray (swan river) everlasting, pale pink clover and blue cornflowers; a silver christening mug with ice-cool gypsophila (baby's breath), silver-and-cream carline thistle, silver foliage and pink rosebuds; a brass preserving pan glittering in the hearth with a high-on-texture collection of bulrushes, dried mushrooms, moss and exotic seedheads; a galvanized bucket or watering can filled with bunches of multi-coloured statice and sea lavender – the partnerships are endless, and invariably sympathetic.

Since dried flower containers do not need to be waterproof, damaged finds in junk shops are entirely suitable. Keep a lookout for containers of all kinds. Cream jugs, milk cans, beakers, goblets, troughs, boxes, tins, tea caddys and weighing scales all have a decorative potential in the eyes of an imaginative flower arranger.

To take full advantage of all its glitter potential, the metal should be well polished, and, after cleaning, rubbed with a soft cloth. If crumpled wire-mesh netting is used as a stem holder, the container should be protected from scratches by a thick band of tape stuck around the inside of the rim, or by slivers cut from a block of foam.

PORCELAIN, CHINA AND POTTERY CONTAINERS

Pieces of porcelain, china and pottery have a slightly limited appeal as flower containers. Those with an intricate or delicate pattern can seem at odds with dried materials, and need

ABOVE *Because dried flower arrangements do not require water they can be arranged in hanging bouquets, wicker baskets, or in non-watertight boxes or weathered wood.*

to be used with care. A rose-patterned teapot, for example, may look prettier when arranged with a bunch of roses than with a mixed and more complex medley of several flower types. A blue-and-white ginger jar may look more effective when arranged with a flourish of white or blue flowers than with mixed colours. A modern pottery bowl richly patterned with splashes of primary colours is best arranged with flowers echoing a single colour, or with neutral tones of cream or white.

One of the most effective of china containers is a white pedestal vase, which you can often find in second-hand shops. It lifts the flowers high off the table surface and heightens the interest factor. You could arrange such a container with dyed glixia (star flower), green grasses, gypsophila (baby's breath) and roses. When you are cutting rose stems short to arrange them close to the foam there is no need to waste the dried leaves. Cut them from the stems, wire them together in clusters and insert them among the flowers for a refreshingly natural look.

Glazed and unglazed pottery in all the earthy brown and green shades is a perfect foil for dried flowers and other materials. A tall jug arranged with bulrushes and teasels looks well on a hall table. A beaker brimming over with decorative grasses is a perfect decoration for a kitchen and a flower pot fanning out with a mixture of brown, cream and golden tones is an appropriate display for a hearth or covered porch.

GLASS CONTAINERS

Some of the prettiest flower containers around are made of coloured glass; they may be bowls, beakers, mugs, drinking glasses or vases. Opaque glass has the advantage that it hides the plant stems and does not need camouflage tactics such as a lining of moss or pot pourri (see page 44). The reflective glass, like metal, is flattering to the matt appearance of dried flowers. Careful colour co-ordination is essential if the flowers and container are to look completely unified, and one flower type should echo the colour of the glass as accurately as possible. A group of three red trumpet-shaped glasses arranged with vibrant everlastings as a table centrepiece; a blue and green petal vase arranged with bells-of-Ireland and cornflowers for a dressing-table – coloured glass and dried flowers have an especially decorative relationship.

WOODEN CONTAINERS

Wooden containers have a wide application in dried flower design. You can use salad bowls, bread boards, cheese boards, a slice across a tree trunk, beakers, tankards, cutlery

AIRTIGHT ARRANGEMENTS FOR BATHROOMS

Dried flowers do not like a steamy atmosphere, and will survive in a bathroom only if it is well ventilated. In a room that suffers from high humidity you can overcome the problem by placing the flowers in an airtight container. Choose a clear, glass-lidded storage jar and place a cardboard tube inside it. Push dried helichrysum (strawflower) heads into the cavity between the tube and the glass, arranging them in neat rings of different colours. Finish with one large flower on top of the tube, put on the lid and tie a ribbon round the neck of the jar. Alternatively, cut a cardboard circle to fit the base of a wide-necked jar. Press a blob of adhesive clay on to it and arrange an elongated design of flowers and foliage, taking care to conceal the holding material. Lower the arrangement into the jar and put the lid on a design that is now steamproof.

trays and lidded boxes, plant trays, garden trugs, plant troughs and hollowed logs for a wide range of designs to display all around the house. The wood may be polished or un-polished, sun-bleached and faded or painted. Whatever the finish, wooden containers take well to a mixed display of dried flowers. A mahogany teabox, for example, its lid propped open, looks luxurious with the aper-ture brimming with a tumbling display of buttercups, roses, clarkia, marjoram, hy-drangea and lady's mantle – a rich-looking medley in jewel colours. A hollowed log makes a perfect container for a porch or sun-room, the top wedged with a block of foam and arranged with, say, bunches of statice, wheat, golden rod and sea lavender. And a wooden bread board makes a perfect base for an upright design composed in a hidden plastic saucer of foam. The arrangement could have a candle as a focal point, with fir cones, reed mace seedheads, lotus flower seedheads, skeletonized leaves and pressed autumn leaves to give a textural balance. For a festive oc-casion, the materials could be spatter-sprayed with gold paint.

CARING FOR YOUR ARRANGEMENTS
~

Dried flower arrangements will give you pleasure for many months or even years as long as they are kept in favourable conditions. As we have seen, they will not tolerate exces-sive dampness in the atmosphere – they re-asbsorb moisture and soon go mouldy – and so steamy kitchens and bathrooms are out of bounds to all but the hardiest of seedheads.

Strong light is the other enemy. Dried flowers look enchanting on a sunny window-sill catching every shaft of the sun. But the sun will soon draw out the colour from the flowers and fade them, pinks and blues alike, to a pale cream.

For this reason it is advisable to place dried

CANDLE TIP

There are two ways of inserting a candle into foam without breaking up the holding material. One is to use a purpose-made plastic spike, available from florists. The other is to tape four matchsticks or wooden cocktail sticks around the base of the candle, with the slivers of wood extending about ¾in (2cm) below the candle. Push the matchsticks into the foam and the candle will rest on top of it, without making a hole.

---

flower designs in a part of the room that does not catch direct sunlight. If this happens to be a dark corner of the room, select flowers in pale colours – soft yellows, pinks and cream – that will show up well, and brightly.

When in the fullness of time you may tire of a flower arrangement and feel in need of a change, or when you start lighting fires and make the fireplace display redundant, you can take the design apart and re-use the materials. Dismantle the arrangement carefully, stem by stem, and ruthlessly discard any faded or damaged flowers. Cut off any florets or leaves that have been squashed or broken and gen-erally trim and tidy up stems. Store the re-maining "good" flowers between tissues in a box, or standing upright in a container until you are ready to use them again.

If a flower arrangement begins to look rather dusty and lacks its original personality, take it to an open window and, very gently, blow off the dust using a hair dryer on the coolest, slowest setting. Appraise the arrange-ment, and replace any stems which have lost their colour. It might amount to only half a dozen new flowers, but these could make all the difference, prolonging the life of the ar-rangement for several months to come.

Making a Moss or Hay Wreath

You can cover a wire ring with dry sphagnum moss or hay to create a good-looking, country-style wreath base, useful for a whole range of floral displays.

1 Tie the wire or twine to the outer ring of the frame. Take a handful of moss or hay and wrap it around the back and front of the ring. Bind it over and over with the twine, pulling it tightly to bury it.

YOU WILL NEED

Copper-wire ring frame; the one shown is the "dished" type, 10in (25cm) in diameter

Roll of fine silver wire or you can use twine for binding

Dry sphagnum moss or hay

Scissors

2 Add more moss or hay and bind it on all around the ring until the frame is completely covered.

3 The ring frame covered with moss can now be used as a natural-looking base for decorations of evergreens, dried flowers, and herbs.

The decorative materials should be wired and the wires pushed through the moss to the back of the frame and secured there.

The Projects

Floral decorations are so much associated with festivals and celebrations of all kinds that it is tempting to think of them only on special occasions – which would be a great pity, for they are a glorious opportunity for self-indulgence all year round!

This sections offers ideas for floral arrangements that draw on traditional inspirations, as well as designs with a distinctly modern feel. Some are composed entirely of dried flowers, while others use fresh materials that could be left to dry naturally, to be treasured for a longer time.

Many of the designs described here use scented flowers and foliage; keep this in mind when deciding where to put your completed arrangement. It may be doubly effective on a low table where its aroma can evoke thoughts of golden fields at harvest time or the fragrance of a traditional herb garden.

You may already have in mind a corner of your home that needs brightening with flowers; or you might be looking for the first spark of inspiration to start off your own ideas. Here, the projects are arranged in chapters according to their form – from posies and wreaths to pomanders and indoor trees – followed by a chapter focusing on designs using nuts, herbs and vegetables, and a special chapter with ideas for festive occasions. If you have a particular purpose in mind, you can quickly find a design to suit.

LEFT *The strength of the three primary colours in this Rainbow Palette (page 69) add to the vibrancy of the arrangement.*

Bouquets and Posies

Flowers gathered into simple bunches or shaped into stylish bouquets have been carried and worn at festivals or festivities and given as tokens of affection, esteem or gratitude since earliest times. Whatever the mood and whatever the occasion, a bouquet or a posy of flowers can have a part to play.

Posies and bouquets come in all shapes and sizes and have many applications. There is the Victorian-style posy composed of a number of concentric rings around a central flower. Because of its romantic and nostalgic associations, such a traditional style is often first choice for a wedding day. Others are less formally arranged, the flowers cascading in a free-fall way, with no clearly defined shape, just an attractive outline. The prettiest free-style bouquets draw their components from three groups of flower shapes: spiky, round and lacy. Think of a posy firstly as a flower arrangement without a container, and you will see that the long spires outline the design and draw in the extremities. The full, round flowers provide weight at the heart of the design, and the lacy materials provide a softening influence.

Some bouquets are designed to be laid on a flat surface; others are designed to hang on furniture or furnishings, in an alcove or on a door. Think of where your arrangement will be used before deciding on the design that suits your purpose.

ABOVE *This bouquet is ideal for weddings, christenings, and birthdays alike, with its pale and delicate colour scheme.*

Tussie-mussie

In England in the Middle Ages and later, people sweetened the air around them by carrying little nosegays of aromatic leaves and flowers, charmingly called tussie-mussies. Today, these posies are appreciated as much for their visual appeal as for their fragrance.

1 To make a shower or cascade posy, place the longest stems flat on the working surface. The lemon balm and lemon mint will both frame and protect the flowers. Arrange the flowers over the leaves, graduating the length of the stems. When you are halfway through, bind the stems with silver wire to keep them in place.

YOU WILL NEED

Florists' scissors

Roll of florists' silver wire

Open-weave ribbon 1½in (4cm) wide

Scissors

Selection of leaves such as lemon balm, lemon mint and sweet cicely

Selection of flowers such as roses, feverfew, sweet peas, marguerite daisies and lady's mantle

2 Arrange some of the lightest materials – in this case sweet cicely leaves and lady's mantle flowers – at the sides of the design and place the main feature flower, a rose, close to the "grip". Bind the stems with wire and then with ribbon.

Glistening Glass

Transparent containers often look unattractive with unsightly stems. Here, the problem is solved with an arrangement that sits on a saucer on top of the vase.

1 The glass vase is
fitted with a
white plastic saucer,
held in place with a
ring of adhesive clay.
The small cylinder of
dry foam exactly fits
into an indent in the
saucer.

2 Short stems
of honesty,
echoing the pattern
on the vase, are
positioned to form a
triangular shape.

YOU WILL NEED

Glass container

Foam-holding plastic

Saucer

Adhesive clay

Small cylinder of dry foam

Honesty

Eryngium (sea holly)

Apricot statice

White sea lavender

Apricot helichrysums (strawflowers)

Blue larkspur

3 The spiky
outlines of the
eryngium (sea holly)
contrast effectively
with the smooth
discs of honesty.

4 Apricot statice introduces a warm colour to the design. The foreground is filled with white sea lavender.

5 The round, full faces of the apricot helichrysums (strawflowers) stand out against the contrasting shapes which form the basis of the design. The blue larkspur follows the outlines and intensifies the colour value.

Chinese Yellow

An oriental feel is created by using cornflower blues and clear golden tones in this simple yet elegant design.

1 The blue and white china bowl is fitted with a trimmed block of dry foam taped from side to side with florists' adhesive tape.

YOU WILL NEED

China or pottery bowl

Block dry foam

Florists' adhesive tape

Blue preserved eucalyptus leaves

Cream helichrysums (strawflowers)

Blue cornflowers

Golden helichrysums (strawflowers)

Yellow achillea (yarrow)

Blue eryngium (sea holly)

2 Blue preserved eucalyptus forms the basis of the design. Some of the stems are cut short so that the leaves nestle close against the foam and help conceal it.

3 Cream helichrysums (strawflowers), contrasting strikingly with the eucalyptus in every way, are recessed into the design. The bright deep blue of the cornflowers echoes the colour of the bowl.

4 With their intense colouring, the golden helichrysums (strawflowers) give an Oriental look to the design. They are positioned to increase the height of the flower dome beneath the outline of the leaves.

5 The flat flower heads of the yellow achillea (yarrow) and the indefinite outlines of the misty blue eryngium (sea holly) add to the textural interest of the design while keeping within the two-colour scheme.

A Tapestry of Colour

These vibrant colours could be used to add zest in a neutral colour scheme. They need to be effectively lit,
so that the darker tones do not get lost in shadow.

1 The neck of the blue and white jug is filled with a mound of crumpled chicken wire held in place by florists' adhesive tape.

YOU WILL NEED

Tall vase or pitcher (jug)

Chicken wire

Florists' adhesive tape

Blue larkspur

Mauve statice

Red rosebuds

Red miniature roses

Dried purple sage leaves

2 With the tallest stems at the centre and the shortest ones at the side, the blue larkspur is arranged to form a rough fan shape.

3 The statice is arranged among the larkspur to add deep blocks of colour.

4 Some extending almost to the uppermost tip and others angled low over the container rim, the roses distribute their colour brightness evenly throughout the design.

5 In such a rich tapestry of colour, the neutral tone of the dried sage leaves strikes the perfect balance. Notice how the leaves are placed not only at the base but on each side of the design.

Baskets of Flowers

A slatted basket filled to over-flowing with a mixture of dried hay, marjoram flowers and lady's mantle; a basket given the air of a rugged log cabin with a covering of cinnamon sticks — baskets of flowers,  herbs and spices have long had a decorative part to play in the home. It is a tradition that has its roots in country lore around the world and one that has been taken up and adapted by modern craftspeople and designers.

As a token of appreciation to your hosts, a basket of fresh or dried flowers, thoughtfully arranged, has all the appeal of the more traditional bouquet while being quite original. And, of course, if you choose dried flowers, they will provide a long-lasting pleasure.

The techniques required to transform a basket could not be simpler nor the materials more homely. Most people have an unused basket tucked away in a cupboard somewhere, just waiting to be given a new lease of life. Give a not-so-special basket a completely new look: a pair or group of matching or assorted baskets may give added impact to your decor. If you use a natural colour basket, consider spraying it a glossy white or pastel that coordinates with your decor and the colour of your flowers.

ABOVE *In this Country Basket (page 74), golden wheat stalks are set off to perfection by the blues of larkspur and the varying pinks of rhodanthe and helichrysums (strawflowers).*

Rainbow Palette

Such a simple arrangement would be an ideal way to quickly brighten up a hallway, or create a spur-of-the-moment gift if you are visiting friends.

1 No fixing material is needed for this design. The flowers are tied into thick bundles of a single colour, the stems cut short so that the lowest flower heads just rest on the rim of the basket.

YOU WILL NEED

Basket

Raffia or twine

Selection of blue-dyed flowers

Selection of yellow flowers

Selection of green-dyed flowers and grasses

Selection of red flowers

2 First the blue, then the yellow and now the pale green – the blocks of colour build up, each one complementing the other.

3 The finished design, with the four bunches of dyed and everlasting flowers in place. It is one of the simplest to create, and can be carried out with any combination of colours.

Posy Basket

Best seen from above to appreciate its fan-like arrangement, this design could be kept on a low table or set at an angle on a kitchen bench.

1 A plastic prong is secured to the base of the basket with a dab of adhesive clay. Then the small piece of foam, cut from a large block, is impaled on the spikes.

YOU WILL NEED

Flat shallow basket

Plastic prong

Adhesive clay

Piece of dry foam

Blue paper ribbon

Stub wire

Golden wheat

Yellow rosebuds

Blue larkspur

Blue broom bloom

White feverfew

Yellow achillea (yarrow)

2 First to be arranged in this illusionary posy design are the heads of golden wheat, their stems cut in short and graduated lengths.

3 Yellow rosebuds are positioned between the wheat, some with their stems cut so short that the flowers nestle against the holding foam.

4 Blue larkspur, adding an intensity of colour, is arranged to fill in the spaces. Again, many of the stems are cut to very short lengths.

5 Now the illusion grows. The posy stalks, all cut from wheat, are positioned in the other side of the foam to make a fan shape. Some extend just beyond the rim.

6 The posy is built up: blue broom bloom and white feverfew both complement the colour scheme and provide a contrast of shape.

7 A few short stems of yellow achillea (yarrow) are inserted between the rosebuds and then the bow is added, a flourish of paper ribbon mounted on a bent stub wire.

Basket of Roses

You can make a ring of roses, pansies, and other midsummer flowers to cascade over the sides of a rustic basket, a pretty country-style decoration for a fireplace, patio, or porch. It's a way of making a few flowers look like a million dollars!

YOU WILL NEED

Round, shallow basket

Absorbent foam ring; ours was 10in (25cm) in diameter

Florists' scissors

Trails of greenery, such as variegated mint, periwinkle, lamium

Roses

Nasturtiums

Cornflowers

Pansies

Marjoram flowers

1 Check that the foam ring fits neatly inside the rim of the basket. Put the leaves and flowers in water before arranging them in the foam. Soak the foam ring in water for several minutes until it is completely saturated.

2 Position the sprays of leaves in the foam ring with short lengths to cover the inner rim and longer stems to trail over the outer one. Place the foam ring in the basket again to check that the leaves will cascade attractively. For a casual look, position the stems close to the top of the foam.

3 Position the roses, the largest of the flowers in the design, around the ring, with some close to the inside and some towards the outside of the ring. Alternate the colours, pale and deep pink, evenly.

4 Fill in the design, grouping several nasturtiums and cornflowers together to create maximum impact. It may be necessary to push a hole in the foam, using a match or stub wire, to position the slender stems of the pansies. Fill in the gaps with short lengths of marjoram, a flower that allows all the others to take the limelight. Place the ring in the basket again, and check that the foam is completely covered. The basket should look full to overflowing with midsummer glory!

Country Basket

It may be an old but now discarded favourite or one that you picked up in a charity shop, or it may just not fit in with your current scheme of things – but here is a way to give a not-so-special basket a completely new look.

YOU WILL NEED

Florists' scissors

Basket

Glue gun

Paper ribbon

Half a stub wire

Scissors

Raffia

Dried herbs such as marjoram and lady's mantle

Dry hay or sphagnum moss

Fresh herbs and flowers such as marigolds, cornflowers, larkspur, mint and marjoram

Jars of herbs and spices, herbed vinegars and biscuits

1 You can use any dried herbs from your collection to make a fragrant mixture. Choose toning shades of paper ribbon to cover the herb and spice jars and to decorate the basket handle.

2 Strip any leaves from the stalks and cut off the marjoram and lady's mantle flowers. Gently mix them with the hay, which we have used, or the moss, taking care not to crush the herbs.

3 Working on a small area at a time, cover the basket sides with glue. Leave the glue to cool for a few seconds so that you do not burn your fingers, then press on handfuls of the hay and herb mixture. Surprisingly, the hay mixture will be so enmeshed and intertwined that it should stay in place.

4 Cut a length of paper ribbon and unfurl half of it. Tie it into a bow and fix it to the basket handle with half a stub wire threaded through the back of the loop. Cut the unfurled end slantwise to neaten it.

5 Form the fresh herbs and flowers into a posy, tie the stalks with raffia and cut the ends. Fill the basket with the kind of herb and spice goodies that a friend or relative would love to receive. We chose cinnamon biscuits, caraway biscuits, herbed vinegars, and a selection of dried spices in tiny jars.

Log-cabin Basket

Here is one of the spiciest ideas ever – a cheap and cheerful basket covered with cinnamon stick "logs" and filled to the brim with fresh bright chillies.

1 This long-forgotten basket had worked its way to the back of a cupboard and did not look too promising, but that was before it was given the log-cabin treatment!

2 Measure the cinnamon sticks against the depth of the basket and cut them to length. The off-cuts can be used for cooking. Any joins will be hidden by the raffia band. Use the glue gun to spread a strip of glue from top to bottom of the basket. Allow the glue to cool for a moment, then press on a cinnamon stick. Work all around the basket until it is covered. Put a few dabs of glue around the centre, press the raffia braid (plait) in place and tie it firmly.

YOU WILL NEED

Straight-sided basket

Florists' scissors

Glue gun

Raffia braid (plait)

Ribbon 1½in (4cm) wide

Scissors

Cinnamon sticks

Fresh chillies

3 Tie ribbon bows around the handle and cut the ribbon ends slantwise. We chose red and green tartan ribbon to combine the colours of the chillies. Fill the basket with chillies and a few more cinnamon sticks for good measure.

Festive Wreaths and Garlands

Wreaths and garlands have a long history and a deep symbolism. From the earliest time and throughout the world, floral and herbal rings have been hung on doors as signs of welcome, and new homes were adorned with wreaths to signify good fortune. The tradition and the craft of making garlands and wreaths live on and are as relevant today as they ever were. In a spur-of-the-moment dash of enthusiasm, it is still possible, and remarkably simple, to make wreath and garland bases from the natural materials all around us.

If a short-cut offers more appeal, however, you can now get your designs off to an instant start by taking advantage of the wide range of ready-made bases that are available in florists, craft shops and department stores. You will find a variety of fine wreath forms and twisted stem circles, preformed shapes of dry and absorbent stem-holding foam, and braided (plaited) straw or raffia rings and swags. The twisted-twig wreath bases come in all sizes and are made from a variety of materials: stout and shiny brown willow twigs, or parchment-coloured bleached willow; rugged rings of knobbly vine; lover's knot and heart-shaped ones to inspire romantic floral designs; and thick country-style rings of tightly packed stems covered with a decorative top layer of dried grasses. No matter what style of wreath you are creating, there is a base to suit your needs.

ABOVE *This Peony Ring (page 92) is a romantic tribute to summer, with dried peonies, cream-coloured rosebuds, poppyheads and dried herbs.*

Midsummer Table Ring

Capture the essence of summer with this highly scented table decoration. To give it extra pizazz, you could replace the cluster of tapers with sparklers.

YOU WILL NEED

Floral foam ring soaked in water; ours was
10in (25cm) in diameter

Florists' scissors

Tapers or sparklers

Scissors

Selection of herb leaves such as scented
geranium and variegated mint

Selection of flowers such as feverfew, lady's
mantle and pinks

Caraway seedheads

1 You can select herbs and flowers to match a specific colour scheme – lime green, yellow and white, for example – or go for a more random look and include flowers in all the colours of the rainbow.

2 Begin by concealing the foam ring beneath a layer of herb leaves. We used individual scented geranium leaves and small sprays of variegated mint to give the design a light, bright look. Add small sprays of lady's mantle.

3 Add the bright daisy-like shapes of the feverfew, cutting the stems short so that the lowest flowers lie close against the foam. Add the caraway seedheads at intervals around the ring.

4 Cut short lengths from the base of some of the tapers and arrange them in a group at one side of the ring. Arrange the pinks in a cluster among them.

5 When the tapers are alight and flickering in a light summer breeze, this will be a delightful table decoration for a midsummer garden party.

Flower-decked Hat

*Encircle a favourite straw hat with scented leaves, stud it with a galaxy of flowers and it will be all set
for a country wedding, either as highly individual headgear or as a pretty summer wall decoration.
Adhesive clay is available from most florists' shops.*

1 Cut a few strands of raffia, wrap them around the brim of the hat and tie them in a secure knot. Cut short the ends.

2 Remove the raffia band. Cut short stems of marjoram and love-in-a-mist and slightly longer ones of chives. Gather three or four chives, a stem of marjoram and one of love-in-a-mist into a cluster and bind them to the raffia band with silver wire. Continue all around the band until it is covered completely.

3 Slip the band over the crown of the hat. Cut several strands of raffia to a length of about 10in (25cm) and tie them around the band to make an unruly "bow".

4 Break off small pieces of the clay. Cut the stems from the pinks and cornflowers and use pieces of clay to stick them in random order around the brim of the hat.

5 Because the flowers take only moments to arrange, it is best to leave this stage of the decoration until the last minute so that the flowers can stand in water as long as possible. Trim them and arrange them just before the event.

Floral Drapes

There's nothing like a flowery garland to transform a piece of furniture, an alcove, a doorway, fireplace or pillar and to set the scene for a party. This garland, which is composed of a blend of herb leaves and flowers, is enhanced by the romantic aroma of pot pourri.

1 Measure the rope or cord across the area to be decorated allowing for gentle drapes and side trails. Slice a block of soaked foam in half lengthways and cut it into pieces about 1½in (4cm) thick. Hold pieces of foam on either side of the rope to make a rope "sandwich" and bind them in place with the twine. Attach pieces of foam along the rope, leaving a gap of about 2in (5cm) between them.

YOU WILL NEED

Rope or stout cord

Floral foam, soaked in water

Knife

Green binding twine

Florists' scissors

Stub wire

Wire cutters

Paper ribbon

Scissors

Selection of flowers such as lady's mantle, marjoram, feverfew and cotton lavender

Fennel seedheads

Selection of leaves such as bay and mint

2 Begin the garland with your most plentiful – or inexpensive – plant material. We covered the foam with short sprays of lady's mantle, then added fennel seedheads, and finally added the glossy contrast of bay leaves.

3 Add the more decorative materials, the yellow domes of cotton lavender flowers, the clusters of daisy-white feverfew and the purple and mauve marjoram and mint. Hold the garland against a wall to check that there are no gaps or tell-tale glimpses of foam or rope. Add more herb sprays if there are.

4 Because it is constructed on a base of foam blocks, the garland will hang in easy, pretty drapes. Cut stub wires in half and bend each length into a U-shaped staple. Unfurl the paper ribbon, tie it into bows and fix one to each "point" of the garland. Trim the ends slantwise.

Greek May Day Ring

Capture the joy of the Greek springtime festival, protomayia, *by making a colourful flower ring, known as a* stefani, *for the front door.*

1 Simplicity is the keynote of these traditional country-style rings which are made with natural materials. A handful of bryony stems forms the core of the wreath. You can choose raffia or green twine both to bind the core and to bind on the flowers. As the flowers will have no moisture source, give them a good long drink before commencing the design.

YOU WILL NEED

Raffia or twine

Scissors

Florists' scissors

Supple stems, such as bryony, weeping willow or cow parsley

Selection of brightly coloured fresh wild and cultivated flowers, such as poppies, cornflowers, marigolds, spray chrysanthemums, marguerite daisies, feverfew, sweet peas and nasturtiums

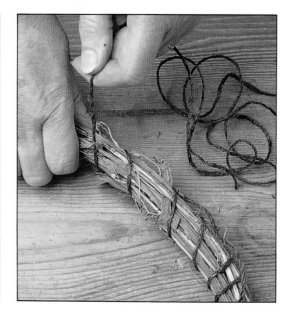

2 Gather the stems neatly and form them into a tightly packed strip. Secure the binding material at one end and bind it round and round the stems, pulling it tightly as you do so. Any leaves still attached to the stems are bound in, and just add to the informality. Overlap the stem ends slightly, and bind them together. Ease the core to make a neat circular shape.

3 Bind on small flowers in mixed bunches, large ones singly or in pairs. Do not try to even out the colours or balance the flower shapes around the ring. The charm of designs of this kind is their air of spontaneity.

4 Continue binding on more flowers around the ring, the heads of one cluster covering the stems of the previous one. If a little of the ring base shows in the finished design it will not in any way detract from the pastoral effect.

5 When you have completed the ring, spray the flowers with a fine mist of cool water, and repeat this several times a day, especially in hot weather. In Greece the flower rings are left on the doors for several weeks, and they gradually fade.

Floral Table Swag

Whether it's a wedding in a public hall, a christening tea party in the garden, or some other special family celebration, a floral swag draws flattering attention to the table and sets the scene for a memorable occasion. This one is composed, somewhat unusually, of asparagus fern, variegated mint and hollyhock flowers.

1 The delicate effect of this swag is achieved by using light-looking foliage and flowers – feathery and variegated leaves and pale-coloured flowers with an attractive trumpet shape. For an occasion like this, solid, dark green foliage could make the design look too wintry. If you pick separate hollyhock flowers from several plants, to avoid cutting whole stems, float them in a bowl of water.

2 Measure the string to give a gentle curve across the table front. Each side of the table is decorated with a separate swag. Place one stem each of asparagus fern and mint over the string close to one end and bind it in place by taking the roll wire over and around the stems and string two or three times. Bind the foliage stems all the way along and bind on a hollyhock flower at intervals.

3 Bind on more foliage, the asparagus fern and mint together, to make a continuous line. Trim off any particularly wayward pieces (of the fern especially) that would spoil the line of the swag. Fasten off the wire by tying it close to the end of the string. Make further swags in a similar way for each side of the table, reversing the direction the flowers face on alternate swags.

4 Tie the ribbon close to one end of the swag and bind it round and round between the flowers and over the foliage stems. Do not pull it too tightly; it looks prettier in soft folds. Tie the ribbon close to the other end of the swag.

5 The gentle fall of the swag in close-up. Crisp white cotton is the perfect and traditional backing, though the design would look equally effective on a pastel-coloured cloth.

6 Tie the free ends of the string together, and pin the swags to each corner of the table, slightly adjusting the length if necessary to make sure that the drape is even. Make four ribbon bows and pin one to each corner, to hide the joins and make a pretty focal point.

YOU WILL NEED

Thick string

Roll of fine silver wire

Scissors

Florists' scissors

White-headed pins

Ribbon 1in (2.5cm) wide

Asparagus fern, or another "feathery" foliage such as maidenhair fern

Variegated mint or another variegated foliage such as periwinkle or lamium

Hollyhock flowers; or you could use roses or mallow (lavatera)

Strawberry Fair

When you are planning the table decorations for a summer party, let your imagination run riot! There is no need to confine your designs to flowers alone – luscious soft fruits can be used to most delectable effect.

1 Soak the foam ring in water for several minutes, until it is completely saturated. As an alternative, you could make a ring of foam slices arranged around a plate, as described in the Easter table ring project on page 151, and fill the dish in the centre with more strawberries.

YOU WILL NEED

Absorbent foam ring; ours was 12in (30cm) in diameter

Florists' scissors

Wooden cocktail sticks

Strawberries, about 12oz (350g)

Lady's mantle

Cornflowers

2 Look over the strawberries, and put aside any blemished ones which would detract from the look of the design. Cut short stems of lady's mantle and arrange them, with a few of the leaves, around the ring, to cover not only the top but the inner and outer rims as well.

3 Complete the covering of the ring with the base material, the yellowy-green and fluffy sprays of the lady's mantle which form a soft background to the more showy materials. Arrange cornflowers all around the ring, not forgetting the inner and outer rims.

4 Spear the base of each strawberry with a cocktail stick. By attaching the fruit in this way, it is not harmed, and can be eaten when the design is dismantled.

5 Arrange the strawberries evenly around the ring so that their stems rise just above the level of the lady's mantle. Check that no traces of the foam ring can be seen, and fill in any gaps with more flower or leaf sprays.

6 With the deep, clear blue of the cornflowers and the scarlet red of the strawberries in place, the vibrant effect achieved by combining two primary colours can be clearly seen. Play up to this bold, bright look by displaying the decoration on a strong matching colour such as a dark blue or brilliant red cloth.

Outdoor Party Garland

Whatever the occasion, you can brighten any venue by introducing flowers. Make our floral ribbon garland to hang beneath a windowsill, across a garden gate or from tree to tree in a midsummer gesture that says "welcome".

1 Choose the colour of the coiled paper ribbon, which forms the core of the garland, to contrast well with the background and to complement the flowers. A pale colour shows to advantage against a black weather-boarded wall. A dark colour would have more impact on a white gate. Revive the flowers in cool water.

2 Open out the paper ribbon at intervals where the coil will not be covered with flowers. It is not only more economical in the use of flowers to leave gaps in the garland, but it also gives the design a built-in change of texture. First, measure the required length of the garland, work out where the gaps will be, and mark the areas on the paper coil, then gently ease out the paper between the pencil marks.

3 Divide the flowers into two groups, so that each end of the garland matches the other. Gather the flowers into small mixed bunches, and wire them on to the paper core. Wire each successive bunch so that the flower heads cover the stems of the one before. The paper bows will cover the stems of the bunches on the ends of the garland.

YOU WILL NEED

Coiled paper ribbon

Pencil

Scissors

Roll of fine silver wire

Florists' scissors

Nails or drawing pins for fixing

Selection of long-lasting flowers in white
and bright colours, such as spray
chrysanthemums, cornflowers, scabious,
marigolds, feverfew

4 Open out
enough of the
coiled paper to make
two large ribbon
bows. For a really
full and generous
look, allow about 1
yard (1 metre) for
each. Tie the paper
to make a bow in the
usual way, and cut
the ends slantwise to
neaten them.

5 Fix the garland
in place with
nails, drawing pins,
or similar, and pin a
bow at each end. In
hot weather, if you
spray the flowers
with water, protect
the paper core and
bows from the jet.
And if the guests
have to retreat
indoors in a summer
shower, don't forget
the garland also
needs cover!

Peony Ring

The deep, hazy pink of dried peonies, the pretty luxury of dried cream-coloured rosebuds, the scents of the herb garden and the sensuous feel of sun-dried hay, all come together in a design that pays a romantic tribute to summer. You could display it on a wall, on an occasional table, or in a shallow, rustic basket.

YOU WILL NEED

Flat copper-wire ring; ours was 10in (25cm) in diameter

Twine

Scissors

Stub wires

Florists' scissors

Well-dried hay or dry sphagnum moss

Dried peonies

Dried rosebuds

Dried poppyheads

Dried sea lavender

Dried purple sage leaves

1 Cover the ring thickly on both sides with hay, binding it round and round with twine. The way to do this is shown in the photographs on page 57. Select flowers in the romantic colours of summer: deep and pale pink and cream make a delightful combination.

2 Cut short the stems of the dried flowers. Gather them into full mixed bunches, composed of one peony, a rosebud, a poppyhead, several sprays of sea lavender and several stems of sage. Bind the stems with a stub wire, and twist the two ends of the wire together.

3 To attach the bunches to the hay ring, push the wire ends deep into the hay and through to the back. Bend the wires back over the outer wire circle of the ring. Add more bunches around the ring, positioning some bunches close to the outside and others close to the inside of the ring. As usual, the flower heads of one bunch will cover and conceal the stems of the one before.

4 The decoration is designed to leave one section of the tactile hay uncovered, but you could complete the ring by adding more bunches.

Blue and White Circlet

A plain white jug takes on a new and more romantic personality when it is encircled by a ring of dried flowers. To flatter our lovely Parianware jug, we made a selection of larkspur, love-in-a-mist, ammobium, cornflowers and sea lavender, all in old-fashioned blue and white.

1 The long spires of dried larkspur can be snipped into several short stems to bring them into scale with a small design. The cornflowers, still the brightest of blue, were dried in a microwave.

YOU WILL NEED

Dry foam ring; ours was 6in (15cm) in diameter; or you can make one by cutting the shape in two halves from a block of dry foam

Florists' scissors

Dried larkspur

Dried cornflowers

Dried love-in-a-mist

Dried ammobium

Dried sea lavender

2 Cut short lengths of larkspur and position them close together all around the top and outer side of the ring, leaving the inside clear. Cut short lengths of the other flowers.

3 Fill in the ring with the other materials, keeping an even colour balance all the way round. The design looks more natural if some stems of sea lavender, for example, extend a little beyond the circular outline to give a slightly spiky appearance.

4 The jug and its dried flower circlet form part of a still-life group in a chimney alcove. The blue and white theme is echoed in pottery, and bunches of dried lady's mantle, lavender and love-in-a-mist hang beside the chest of drawers.

Lavender Ring

A ring of lavender has gentle connotations reminiscent of a by-gone age, and would make a delightful gift for a venerable aunt or grandmother. Our design, using lavender bunches alternated with the softest, palest mauve statice, would charm the younger generation, too.

YOU WILL NEED

2 stub wires

White gutta-percha tape

Scissors

Roll of fine silver wire

Florists' scissors

Ribbon 1in (2.5cm) wide

Dried statice

Dried lavender

1 The design is composed of a ring made of two stub wires joined together and bound round with white gutta-percha tape. It has a diameter of 7½in (19cm). Choose the palest colour of statice you can find. If you cannot find pastel mauve, use pale pink, pale blue, or white, and choose matching ribbon.

2 Cut short the lavender stems and group them into small bunches. Bind the stems with fine roll wire for easy binding. Cut short sprays of statice and bind them into small bunches. Attach the first lavender bunch to the ring with roll wire, taking it tightly over the stems and round the ring. Do not cut it.

3 Bind on statice and lavender bunches alternately, so that the flower heads of one bunch cover the stems of the one before. Continue binding on flower bunches until the ring is covered. If traces of the wire ring show, tuck extra lavender or statice stems under the roll wire.

4 Tie the ribbon around the ring and over the stems. Tie it into a bow and neaten the ends by cutting them at an angle, slantwise.

5 The finished design could be displayed on a dressing table, hung in a wardrobe, or placed in a drawer to scent lingerie or woollens.

Rosemary for Remembrance

Give one to your Valentine, hang one above a bed or a dressing-table – this dainty, heart-shaped decoration speaks volumes of romance.

1 Although red roses and rosebuds traditionally signify true love, we have broken with tradition and included some cream flowers to lighten the design a little and to give it variety.

YOU WILL NEED

Roll of heavy-gauge wire

Wire cutters

Roll of florists' silver wire

Scissors

Satin ribbon ½in (12mm) wide

Slender sprays of rosemary

Wheat stalks or narrow cane

Dried flowers such as rosebuds, lady's mantle and helichrysums (strawflowers)

2 Twist the wire into a circle. Then, by pinching it at the base and the top, make it into a heart shape. Ours measured 8in (20cm) in length. Cut short sprays of rosemary and bind two or three together on the wire frame with silver wire.

3 Place two wheat stalks together. Cut another stalk into several short lengths and fasten these to the top of the two long stalks. They will form the top of the decoration. Bind short sprays of rosemary and the dried flowers along the length of the stalk, placing the rosebuds so that they face in opposite directions.

4 Tie the ribbon close to the top of the stalks so that it conceals the first stem binding. Fasten the stalk to the top and base of the heart and tuck in small flower sprays to conceal the wires. Wire a single rose to the side of the heart.

5 The rosemary will gradually dry on the decoration if it is hung in a warm, dry atmosphere. Then it will become a lasting token.

6 Pure nostalgia! The heart-shaped design looks dainty and pretty when it is displayed against old lace.

Autumn Glory

A compact arrangement like this one would be an ideal touch in a narrow alcove, or above a small fireplace. It would look lost on too large an expanse of wall.

1 The wall-hanging basket, made of woven dried leaves, is wedged with two blocks of dry foam taped together with florists' adhesive tape. As the foam fits tightly, no fixing materials are necessary.

YOU WILL NEED

Wall-hanging basket

2 blocks of dry foam

Florists' adhesive tape

Preserved leaves

Hogweed seedheads

Teasels

Chinese lanterns

Orange-dyed achillea (yarrow)

Oats

Preserved bells-of-Ireland

2 Sprays of preserved leaves are arranged to form a cross shape. The hogweed seedheads form the centre of the design.

3 Teasels, with their solid oval shapes and soft neutral colouring, begin to fill in the arrangement, their heads outlining a rough triangle.

4 Curving stems of Chinese lanterns, with some of the seedheads still at the pale green stage, follow the lower outlines. Orange-dyed achillea (yarrow), forming solid blocks of colour, fills in the centre.

5 A few wispy stems of oats are added at the sides and in the centre. Bells-of-Ireland, the stems cut short, are placed to fill in the spaces and complement the strong orange colouring.

Trees and Foliage Features

Indoor trees, sometimes called designer trees, make an unusually pretty use of dried flowers. With all the classic style of clipped topiary and all the charm of a dried flower arrangement, such trees can be made as table or floor-standing decorations; it depends on the size of the foam sphere you use.

The trees are made of a foam ball pierced on the end of a "tree trunk" which can be a gnarled twig, a smooth branch, a dried hogweed stem, a dowel wrapped with raffia or a bamboo cane. The dry foam balls which form the heart of the trees are made in sizes from 3in (7.5cm) to 10in (25cm) in diameter.

Your tree support can be planted in ceramic or earthenware pots, in wooden troughs, metal bowls or any other suitable container. You can use well-compacted soil to anchor the support, but florists' clay (for small designs) or plaster of Paris gives firmer results. Cover the top of the container with a layer of granite chippings, pot pourri or moss to hide the holding material.

This chapter also includes a range of suggestions for floral decorations that rely on foliage, stems or grasses as their main ingredient. If you want to use flowercraft to achieve a more subtle, restrained effect, this could be just the way to do it.

ABOVE *In this Golden Flower Tree (page 104) the blue borage offers a striking contrast to the warmth of the bright artemisia.*

Summery Table Garland

Whenever there's a special celebration, highlight the party table with a dried flower garland. There are twin advantages to using preserved flowers. You can achieve a summery look in winter, and you can create the garland well in advance of the occasion.

1 Make your selection of dried flowers. As only short-stemmed flowers are needed, you may be able to use left-over clippings from other designs, or flowers with broken stems. Measure the string, the core of the garland, to go round the perimeter of the table, but allow for tying.

2 Cut short sprays of the sea lavender, which forms a continuous line along the garland. Tie the silver wire close to one end of the string, bind on a few sprays of sea lavender, and then more sprays to cover the stems. Bind on the feature flowers at intervals until the garland is long enough.

YOU WILL NEED

Thick string

Spool of fine silver wire

Scissors

Florists' scissors

White-headed pins

Ribbon 1 inch wide

Dried sea lavender

Dried statice

Dried helichrysums (strawflowers)

Dried rosebuds

Dried peonies

3 Pin one end of the garland to the tablecloth, and pin it at intervals all the way round. Tie the two free ends of the string. Make large double ribbon bows, trim the ends and pin them in place around the table, positioning one to hide the join in the string.

Golden Flower Tree

The great thing about designing your own trees is that you can style them to match your own furnishings, to remember a special occasion or special moment or to bring a splash of sunshine colour into your home. Modelling clay is available in most craft shops and in department stores.

YOU WILL NEED

Flowerpot and stand; our container was 5in (12.5cm) in diameter

Masking tape

Modelling clay or florists' hard-setting clay

Pre-formed floral foam ball, 3in (7.5cm) in diameter, soaked in water

Twig or cane; ours was 12in (30cm) long

Florists' scissors

Pot pourri in toning colour

Corded and satin ribbons ½in (12mm) wide

Selection of flowers such as borage, lady's mantle, golden rod and artemisia

1 Your could use a plain earthenware flowerpot, which would give the design a rustic look, but we chose one that had been painted with blue and then spattered with bright green, two colours that are repeated in the sprays of borage. Cover any drainage holes with masking tape.

2 Shape the modelling clay into a ball, push the end of the twig into it and press the clay into the base of the flower pot. Use more clay if necessary to hold the twig in place.

3 Press the foam ball firmly on top of the twig. Cut short sprays of lady's mantle and arrange them all around the ball as the foundation of the design.

4 Position sprays of bright yellow artemisia flowers and variegated mint all around the ball, then add colour accents of blue borage at intervals. Trim off any unduly wayward ends.

5 Fill the flowerpot with pot pourri. Tie the ribbons around the twig just beneath the ball and cut the ends slantwise to neaten them. Spray the tree with a fine mist of water each day to keep the flowers fresh for as long as possible.

Statice Tree

Using flowers in different tones of the same colour, it is the varied sizes and textures of blooms that make this tree such a pleasure to look at. It would be a lovely windowsill decoration, as shown here.

1 The block of clay is pressed into the base of the pot and the twig pushed into it. The foam sphere, pushed on to the top of the twig, is partly covered with short sprays of white statice.

3 Short lengths of yellow broom bloom are added to the design, the stems slightly longer than those of the statice.

4 Moss is used to fill the pot and cover the holding material, and a bright ribbon bow is tied just below the flower tree.

2 Statice, which is widely available and relatively cheap, is a good choice for the tree. Yellow sprays are inserted among the white flowers until the foam is almost completely covered.

YOU WILL NEED

Earthenware flowerpot

Block of hard-setting clay

Sturdy twig

Dry foam sphere

Green satin ribbon

White statice

Yellow statice

Yellow broom bloom

Sphagnum moss

Country Casual

Foliage is the focus in this spherical design. Because of its shape, it would be best hung from the ceiling so that it can be appreciated from all perspectives.

1 A bent stub wire is pressed into the top of the sphere so that it can be hung on a piece of string. Short, even stems of green wheat are positioned all around the sphere.

2 Green oats, cut to the same length as the wheat, continue to build up the design. In place of the cereals you could use decorative grasses or, for a country garden effect, short stems of lavender.

3 Cream helichrysums (strawflowers) and blue-dyed rhodanthe, the stems cut short and the heads pressed close against the foam, give substance to the design and help to conceal the sphere.

YOU WILL NEED

Dry foam sphere

Stub wire

String

Tartan ribbon

Green wheat

Green oats

Cream helichrysums (strawflowers)

Blue-dyed rhodanthe

Red helichrysums (strawflowers)

Hare's-tail grass

4 Red helichrysums (strawflowers) and the natural, neutral tone of the fluffy hare's-tail grass complete the design – a striking composition of two primary colours. A tartan ribbon is stapled to the string and finished with a flat bow.

A Handful of Stems

Absolutely simple, perfectly stunning: the clean tubes of the hogweed stems are shown off in a simple glass bowl, providing a quirky note in a contemporary decor.

1 The dried hogweed stems, cut to equal lengths, are arranged in a glass fish-bowl vase to form a tightly packed twist.

YOU WILL NEED

Glass fish-bowl vase

Bunch of dried hogweed stems

Lavender

Blue larkspur

Red rosebuds

Red miniature roses

Preserved and bleached eucalyptus leaves

2 First to be positioned in the cluster of hogweed stems are short lengths of lavender, arranged in bunches of six or seven stems.

3 Blue larkspur, cut to match the lavender in length, reinforces the colour and strengthens the mass of near-vertical lines.

4 Red rosebuds and clusters of miniature roses begin to soften the geometric lines of the design and add a bright colour element.

5 Pale cream, translucent eucalyptus leaves bring a third, and contrasting shape to the design. The natural twist and twirl of the leaves is particularly striking against the erect hogweed stems.

Brown Study

One of the attractions of dried flowers is that almost anything can be used as a container or base. Bring a touch of woodland into your home with this simple but effective grouping.

1 Use a wooden bread or cheese board, or a slice cut across a tree trunk. The cylinder of foam is secured on a plastic prong stuck to the board with adhesive clay.

YOU WILL NEED

Wooden board

Plastic prong

Adhesive clay

Small cylinder of dry foam

Bulrushes

Lotus seedheads

Preserved and bleached eucalyptus leaves

Teasels

Dock or sorrel seedheads

2 Five bulrushes are arranged first, to define the height and width of the design.

3 Lotus seedheads, in two sizes, add a touch of the exotic. The larger ones, positioned close to the foam, will help to conceal it.

4 Short stems of
bleached
eucalyptus contrast
strikingly with the
browns and the
sturdy textures of the
other materials.

5 A sunburst of
teasels creates
an inner curve and
forms a colour
balance that links the
pale tints and deep
tones. The design is
finished with the
delicate outlines of
the sorrel seedheads.

Provençal Grass Ring

As wild poppies have such a fleeting decorative life once they are picked, we show a long-lasting alternative, a grass ring emblazoned with the most colourful of everlasting flowers, helichrysums (strawflowers) in zingy red, pink, yellow and orange.

1 Take a handful of grasses and trim the root ends. Divide the grasses in two, placing the heads of one group over the root ends of the other. Tie the twine close to one end and bind it over and over them all along the length. Bring the other end round to form a circle and slightly overlap the first. Bind over the join and tie the twine.

YOU WILL NEED

Twine

Roll of fine silver wire

Scissors

Florists' scissors

Safety matches

Long-stemmed supple grasses to make the core

A selection of grasses of varying types to give as much visual variety as possible

Wild poppies or fresh or dried helichrysums (strawflowers)

2 Cut the decorative grasses into short lengths, about 4½in (11.5cm) long. Divide them into colourful bunches. The most attractive effect is achieved when the grasses range from dark brown through pale beige to pastel green. Bind the stems of each bunch with roll wire.

3 Place one of the grass bunches flat against the ring and bind it securely in position, using roll wire or twine. Place each successive bunch close to the one before, so that the grass heads cover the stems of the previous bunch.

4 To give the wild poppies the best chance of a prolonged decorative life, put them in water (even if it is stream or river water) as soon as they are picked. Burn the stem end of each flower for a few seconds by holding it under the flame of a match. Then put the flowers in water again for as long as the impromptu nature of the design allows.

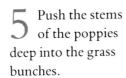

5 Push the stems of the poppies deep into the grass bunches.

6 As an alternative, attach helichrysums (strawflowers) around the ring. To do this, push the flower stems through the strands binding the bunches of grass. With its brilliantly coloured floral decoration, the grass ring makes maximum impact when displayed against an all-the-colours-of-the-rainbow background.

Pot Pourri and Pomanders

Making pot pourri is an extension of the art of drying flowers, and adds another dimension to decorating the home. A bowl of tactile, colourful pot pourri is a delightful and natural way to scent a room. In the Middle Ages, wealthy families throughout Britain and northern Europe employed a lady of the pot pourri whose task it was to preserve fragrant plants throughout the year, and "put them up" in pomanders, bowls and bags to scent the rooms, the linen and the wardrobes.

Traditionally, pot pourri is made of scented flowers such as roses, lavender, jasmine, honeysuckle, freesia and orange blossom, and aromatic leaves such as bay, rosemary, lemon thyme, lemon balm, rose geranium and marjoram. Your spice rack will yield many of the popular spices that give pot pourri the depth of its aroma. These include cardamom, coriander, cinnamon, allspice, mace, nutmeg, cloves and star anise.

To hold the scents of the dried plant materials and spices you need a fixative such as dried orris root powder, which is available from herbalists and some chemists (drug stores). To intensify the aroma you need a few drops of an essential plant oil, such as rose, lemon or neroli.

Pot pourri should be as personal as the scent you choose to wear. Don't be afraid to experiment and adapt the recipes given here to suit your preference.

ABOVE *Varying shades of the same colour can be used to beautiful effect as in this delicate Flower Ball (page 124).*

Dry Pot Pourri

Take a handful of dried rose petals, lavender, bay leaves and rosemary, add a sprinkling of spices and a few drops of oil of roses and you have a romantic and fragrant pot pourri – it really is as simple as it sounds.

1 You can vary the ingredients and the proportion of one to another to suit your own preferences or the materials that are available. Only the orris root powder, which acts as a fixative, has a practical role to play.

YOU WILL NEED

2 cups of dried rose petals

1 cup dried lavender

1 cup dried rosemary

A few bay leaves, crumbled

2 tsp (10 ml) grated nutmeg

1 tbsp (15 ml) ground cinnamon

2 tbsp (30 ml) orris root powder

3-4 drops oil of roses

Dried rosebud, to decorate

3 When all the scents are blended and the spices have lost their "rawness", the pot pourri is ready to be displayed in your prettiest china, glass or silver bowls, or in shells, jars or baskets.

2 Mix the dried ingredients in a bowl with a spoon or your fingers. Pour on a few drops of essential oil – oil of of roses will give a sweet perfume, neroli a hint of orange-blossom freshness, and oil of lavender a note of nostalgia. Transfer the ingredients to a lidded container and store it, away from direct light, for 6 weeks, stirring daily.

Moist Pot Pourri

Making pot pourri by the "moist" method, in which salt is used to draw out the moisture from the fresh leaves and petals, is the traditional method and the one that gave the aromatic blend its name.

1 This colourful pot pourri has an as-you-please quality. You can substitute other seasonal flowers and leaves of your choice. Thyme, mint, marjoram and basil will all add a distinctive aroma to the eventual blend.

YOU WILL NEED

2 cups fresh pink rose petals

1 cup fresh yellow rose petals

1 cup fresh peony petals

1 cup fresh larkspur flowers

1 cup fresh marigold petals

1 cup fresh lemon verbena leaves

3 cups cooking salt

¼ cup ground allspice

¼ cup orris root powder

3 drops each oil of roses and lemon verbena oil

2 Mix together the petals, flowers and leaves. Sprinkle a layer of the fresh materials into a lidded container, then a layer of salt, more flowers and so on, finishing with salt. Cover and set it aside for 2 weeks, by which time the plant materials and salt will have formed a block. Break it up into a bowl, stir in the spices and plant oils and transfer it to a lidded container for another 6 weeks. Stir daily.

3 Transfer the pot pourri, which will no longer be moist but paper-dry and sweetly aromatic, to a favourite container. We chose sparkling glass, which shows the flower and herb blend in all its colourful glory. For an even more dramatic effect you could display two or more types of pot pourri in layers. Their different colours would make a striking decoration.

Herb Ball

Whether you wish to give your kitchen a refreshing aroma, to keep insects at bay or simply to store your culinary herbs in an attractive way, this traditional herb ball is the ideal decoration.

1 For a long-lasting decoration, make your choice from the evergreen herbs – bay, rosemary, sage and purple sage – and from spice seedheads such as caraway, fennel and dill.

YOU WILL NEED

Half a stub wire

Floral foam ball soaked in water; ours was 3in (7.5cm) in diameter

String

Florists' scissors

Satin ribbon ½in (12mm) wide

Scissors

Selection of herbs such as rosemary, bay, sage, purple sage, mint, marjoram and thyme

Caraway seedheads

3 Position the caraway seedheads, which are the highlights of the decoration, more or less evenly around the ball. Remove the string and hang the ball on a ribbon. Tie a bow on top.

2 Bend the stub wire in half to make a staple and push it into the foam ball. Hang the ball on a piece of string while you work on the decoration. Cut the stems to almost equal lengths – a perfectly round decoration would look contrived – and build up the design by mixing the various herbs all the way round.

Rosebud Pomander

Our design for a rosebud pomander brings more than a hint of romance to the traditional concept of a clove orange.

1 Choose the smallest, most compact flowers you can find. Both pink and red rosebuds have romantic connotations, but yellow or cream flowers would be equally pretty.

YOU WILL NEED

Pre-formed floral foam ball; ours was 3in (7.5cm) in diameter

Whole cloves

Florists' scissors

Paper ribbon

Scissors

Pins

Dried pink rosebuds

3 Decorate the pomander with a small bow made from the paper ribbon and pinned in place. You can display the pomander in a bowl of pot pourri or in a basket of lavender, or hang it close to your dressing-table.

2 Stud the foam ball with a few cloves – they will not show – but they will give your finished design the aroma of a pomander. Cut the rose stems to short, even lengths and press them in a neat row into the foam. Continue until the ball is covered. If there are any gaps, which may be caused by the shape and compactness of the dried rosebuds, fill them with cloves.

Pot Pourri and Posy Ring

A bowl of pot pourri, a medley of scented flower petals and tiny leaves, adds a note of nostalgia to any room, and is the most delightful of environmental perfumes. Our design takes the colour, the texture and the aroma of the flower mixture and transforms them into an irresistibly pretty decoration.

YOU WILL NEED

Clear, quick-setting, all-purpose glue

Roll of fine silver wire

Ribbon ½in (12mm) wide

Half a stub wire

Decorative grass-covered stem ring; ours was 7in (18cm) in diameter

Pot pourri, about 4oz (100g)

Dried flowers such as rosebuds, sea lavender, feverfew

1 You can use a dried-foam ring, though it would not be as attractive as one made of natural stems and grasses. If you do use foam, be sure to select a glue which is suitable for use with plastic materials. Choose the pot pourri and match the posy flowers and ribbon to the petal colours.

FRESHENING POT POURRI

If in time the pot pourri on the ring loses some of its fragrance, sprinkle on a few drops of an essential oil, such as attar of roses or neroli, or one of the blended pot pourri oils; and if some of the petals fade slightly, dab on a few spots of glue and press on some more petals, or a few miniature dried rosebuds.

2 Spread a thick layer of glue on the surface of the ring, working on a small area at a time. Make sure that the glue spreads in between the hollows in the ring.

3 Press the pot pourri firmly onto the glue. It is surprising how much will stick. Spread glue on the next area around the ring, press on more pot pourri and so on, until the ring, including the sides, is completely covered.

4 Gather the dried flowers into a posy and cut the stems short. Bind them with a short length of roll wire, then tie the ribbon round them and make it into a bow. Bend the half stub wire into a U-shaped staple, push it over the posy stems and press the wire ends into the ring. Trim the ends of the ribbon by cutting them slantwise.

5 A hand-worked American quilt is the perfect setting for this romantic and pretty pot pourri ring.

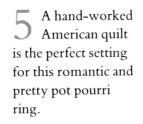

Hearts and Flowers

Pretty pink pot pourri is pressed into service to make a charming table-top decoration, complete with one perfect rose and a twist of ribbon.

1 Cut a piece of paper 8in (20cm) wide and 9in (23cm) long. Fold it in half lengthwise and draw the shape of half a heart and cut it out. Draw a smaller heart shape 4in (10cm) long in the centre and cut it out.

2 Using a knife, cut the foam block in half. Glue the two pieces together along the long sides. Draw around the inner and outer edges of the heart and cut out the foam shape.

YOU WILL NEED

Pencil

Paper

Scissors

Block of dry, stem-holding foam

Knife

Clear quick-setting glue or glue gun

Paper ribbon

Pin

Pot pourri; our design, which was 9in (23cm) long, used about 6oz (150g)

Dried rose

3 Working on a small area at a time, cover the top and sides of the foam heart with glue and press on the pot pourri. If you are using a glue gun, which produces hot glue, leave it to cool for a few seconds to avoid burning your hand. Continue until the foam shape is covered with pot pourri. Glue on more petals or tiny dried flowers to fill in any gaps.

4 Tie the coiled paper ribbon into a bow and stick it to the heart with a pin. Stick the rose in the centre.

5 The pot pourri decoration should hold its scent for several weeks. As the aroma gradually fades you can revitalize it by sprinkling on a few drops of essential flower oil such as rose oil or neroli. A slight fading of the petals and flowers can be quickly remedied – just stick on a few more brightly coloured ones.

Flower Ball

With its delicate blend of silver-green herbs and pale pink flowers, this pretty decoration would be appropriate for a wedding, a baptism or an anniversary celebration.

1 The artemisia leaves, with their pale, silvery-grey colouring and pungent aroma, are used to create the outline of the herb and flower ball. The other scented leaves, which have bolder, more positive shapes, are used as contrasting fillers.

2 Bend the stub wire in half to make a staple and push it into the foam ball. Thread a piece of string through the staple so that you can hang up the ball while you work. Cut the stems of the herbs to an almost uniform length; the flower stems should be a little shorter. Build up the design by pushing the herb stems into the foam, turning the ball around and spacing the stems evenly.

YOU WILL NEED

Half a stub wire

Floral foam ball soaked in water; ours was 3in (7.5cm) in diameter

String

Florists' scissors

Satin ribbon ½in (12mm) wide

Scissors

Selection of herbs and leaves such as artemisia, marjoram, sage, mint and rosemary

Selection of flowers such as roses, pinks, sweet peas, everlasting peas and feverfew

3 Arrange the flower stems so that the shapes are evenly distributed through the design, alternating the full, rounded shapes of the roses and pinks with sprays of sweet pea and everlasting pea. Remove the string and hang the ball on a ribbon tie.

From the Kitchen

Thoughts of harvest and thanksgiving prevail in the projects included in this chapter. The harvest festival or harvest thanksgiving has traditionally been celebrated in chapels and churches, on farms and in country homes in gratitude for bountiful crops. Those same crops yield a wealth of decorative materials to make wreaths, garlands and swags that add a special note to the occasion. Sheaves of wheat and barley may form the centrepiece for still-life groups in local churches, and garlands of wheat or oats may be strung across a door or draped to outline a window.

The vivid colours and intriguing shapes of vegetables and fresh herbs should not be

wasted. Decorative as well as functional, they bring a sense of well-being and abundance to your home when included in designs such as those described here.

Many of the ingredients for these designs – herbs, nuts, vegetables and cereals – come from the kitchen. The finished arrangements need not be restricted to that room, though: use the swags to decorate a dining-room dresser, the rings and garlands above a mantelpiece or in an unused fireplace.

Double the impact by making a matching pair. The swags in particular can be much more effective if placed symmetrically on either side of a doorway or within a spacious alcove.

ABOVE *This colourful Herb Wreath (page 140) can be made of fresh materials and left to dry naturally, a scented reminder of summer.*

Thanksgiving Swag

Our Thanksgiving decoration brings together a medley of dried wheat, oats, hops, and grasses, a handful of bright hot chillies, seedheads, and dried flowers. Here the garland outlines a miniature shelf unit in the kitchen, but it is an idea you could adapt, using aubergines and corn-on-the-cob to decorate a dresser or a doorway.

1 Measure the string to drape over and around the piece of furniture to be decorated and tie a knot in it to mark the centre. (To decorate a large piece of furniture, using heavy vegetables and fruits in the garland, you would need to use strong cord or rope as the core material.)

YOU WILL NEED

Thick string

Scissors

Roll of fine silver wire

Flower scissors

Selection of dried wheat, oats, hops, and grasses

Green and red chillies

Dried flowers, such as carthamus

Dried poppyheads

2 Make bunches of the dried materials, including a spray of hops, if available, in each one. Starting from the centre and working outwards, bind the bunches to the string, taking the roll wire over several times to secure each one. Ensure that the cereal and grass heads cover the stems of the one before.

3 Wire several chillies together by taking roll wire round and round the stalks. Our choice of chillies was determined more by colour and shape variation than for any culinary considerations! Bind the groups of chillies to the garland at regular intervals.

4 When you have completed one side of the garland, start again from the centre and, reversing the direction of the stems, work out towards the other side. Take care that the principal items in the design, and especially the bunches of chillies, match on both sides.

5 Place the garland over the unit and fix it if necessary, though usually the weight of the side trails will be enough to keep it in place. Tuck in extra materials such as a few dried flowers or sprays of hops to cover the change of direction in the centre, and make good any gaps.

Kitchen Colour

Gather together the brightest, shiniest herbs and spices you can find – brilliant green and zingy red chillies, purple and white marjoram and toast-brown nutmegs – and make them into a stylish wall decoration for your kitchen.

1 A glue gun makes short work of sticking on the spices. If you do not have one, use an adhesive that will be strong enough to hold such comparatively heavy spices as ginger and nutmeg in place.

2 Cut the herb stems into short lengths and push them between the binding of the wreath form. For the best effect, use two or three stems of rosemary and of marjoram in a cluster, bound together with silver wire.

YOU WILL NEED

Florists' scissors

Roll of florists' silver wire

Vine wreath form; ours was 10in (25cm) in diameter

Raffia

Scissors

Stub wires

Wire cutters

Clear, quick-setting glue or glue gun

Selection of evergreen herbs such as bay and rosemary

Marjoram flowers

Selection of spices such as dried red and green chillies, ginger, cinnamon sticks, nutmegs and star anise

3 Tie three or four cinnamon sticks in bundles with several strands of raffia and trim off the raffia ends. Cut stub wires in half, bend them to make U-shaped staples and push one end under the raffia. Push the wire ends into the wreath form.

4 Stick the chillies in clusters around the ring, arranging them criss-cross style. Glue on the pieces of dried ginger, the nutmegs and lastly the star anise, using this most decorative of spices to create focal points on the cinnamon sticks and ginger.

5 Hang the decoration on a kitchen wall or door, place it on a working surface or use it as a table centrepiece when you invite friends for an informal meal.

Harvest Sheaf

As the last of the cereal crops were gathered in, farmworkers used to weave decorative items as a symbol of continuing prosperity on the land. Our harvest sheaf, composed on a raffia plait, is a tribute to that tradition. Hang it on a door, a pillar or a post, or make a matching pair for a window, doorway or an arch.

1 You can buy or make a thick raffia plait, which is used as the base of the design. Ours was 24in (60cm) long, 2in (5cm) wide and almost 1in (2.5cm) thick. Make your selection of cereals, grasses, and other seedheads with an eye to texture and colour variety.

2 Prepare the materials for the design. Cut a stub wire in half, wrap it around the centre of a nut and twist the ends at the back. You can, if you wish, tie them with raffia. Wrap half a stub wire around the stem of a large poppy seedhead, extending the stem to make it easier to fix.

3 Make mixed bunches of the cereals, grasses, and seedheads by binding the stems with a stub wire and leaving a long end free, as a false stalk. Build up the design by pushing the wired materials firmly into the raffia, and group the nuts, cinnamon sticks and dried flowers in the centre, leaving planned open spaces.

YOU WILL NEED

Thick raffia plait

Stub wires

Wire cutters

Florists' scissors

Raffia

Scissors

Ribbons, ¾in (2cm) wide and 1in (2.5cm) wide

Selection of cereals and seedheads

Selection of nuts

Cinnamon sticks

Dried carthamus flowers or helichrysums (strawflowers)

4 Make bows with the narrower ribbon, bend half a stub wire to make a U-shaped staple, and push it through the loop at the back of the bow. Push the wire into the plait to fix the bows as an integral part of the design. Make a bow from the wider ribbon and fix it to the top of the plait.

5 The texture and colour of the materials, and the different ways in which they attract the light, change throughout the design. Whether you hang it as a wall decoration or display it on an occasional table, the harvest sheaf will be a delightful reminder of the golden days of the season.

Ring of Oats

It's so sensational, the way that sunlight filters through a field of oats, that we decided to recreate the effect in a purely domestic situation. Our ring of oats, which is bound with dried poppyheads for contrast, can be used as a curtain, hung above a fireplace, on a door or a plain, dark wall.

1 Choose a ribbon colour that will contrast sharply with the neutral, sun-bleached shade of the oats and seedheads. Red or blue would also be good choices.

YOU WILL NEED

Flat copper-wire ring; ours was 10in (25cm) in diameter

Gutta-percha tape (optional)

Roll of fine silver wire

Scissors

Florists' scissors

Ribbon 1in (2.5cm) wide

Dried oats

Dried poppyheads

2 If you wish, cover the copper-wire ring with tape. Tie the roll wire to the outer ring. Take four or five stems of oats. Place them over the ring close to the wire, the heads facing outwards. The eventual size of the decoration is determined by the length of stem you use. Take the stem ends through the centre of the ring, and bend them back, in line with the stem tops. Continue binding stems around the ring. Bind poppy stems (shorter than the oats) in a similar way. Trim off excess stem ends at the back.

3 Cover about three-quarters of the ring with oats and poppyheads. Knot one end of the ribbon close to the stems and wind it around the inner and outer rings. Knot the ribbon close to the stems at the other end and cut it off. Tie the remaining ribbon around the top of the ring and tie it into a bow.

4 As you can see, the finished design would be as effective hanging above a fireplace, on a door or a plain dark wall.

Halloween Hoop

If you're giving a party for Halloween, and especially if teenagers have a hand in the arrangements, you will want an eye-catching decoration verging on the outrageous. Our apple and twig ring comes into just that category, and can be made by even the least adept members of the family.

1 The effect of this design is determined to a large extent by the shape and texture of the twigs. Choose the most gnarled and weathered ones you can find. The covering of green growth on the ones we used is specially effective. Polish the apples so that they shine in the candlelight.

YOU WILL NEED

Twisted-twig ring; ours was 12in (30cm) in diameter

Secateurs (pruning shears)

Stub wires

Wire cutters

Knobbly, gnarled twigs, such as from an apple tree

Apples; we used two varieties

2 Bend a stub wire to make a U-shaped staple. Place one of the twigs flat against the ring, so that the branches extend well beyond the circular shape. Press the staple over the twig and into the ring and check that the twig is held securely. Secure the remaining twigs in a similar way.

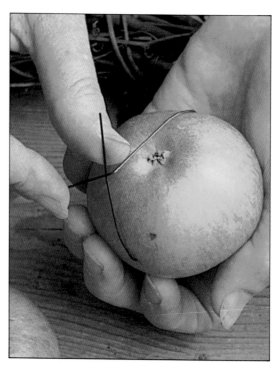

3 Push a stub wire through each apple close to the base, bring the ends together and twist them. Press the twisted wires flat against the apple.

4 Bend a stub wire in half, thread it through the wire at the base of an apple, and press the wire ends at a slanting angle into the twig ring. Check that the apple is firmly held in position. Wire on the remaining ones in a similar way, positioning some around the inside and some around the outside of the ring.

5 The completed ring would never win a prize for neat-and-tidiness, but it will find favour with guests in a party mood. You could hang the ring over a tub of apples bobbing in water – a traditional Halloween game which is still popular.

6 An eye-catching decorative hoop which will certainly impress all who see it.

Culinary Plait

Culinary herbs and spices make a decorative and appealing wall-hanging for a kitchen or dining room.
Make a pair of them to hang on either side of a door, window or fireplace.

1 Even before you begin to assemble the design, you can visualize the colourful impact it will have. Choose a ribbon that will complement both the decor of your room and the natural colours of the ingredients of the plait.

2 Glue four or five nutmegs into a cluster and, when the glue is set, press half a stub wire through one of the spaces between them. Bend the wire to make a U-shaped staple.

YOU WILL NEED

Clear quick-setting glue or glue gun

Stub wires

Wire cutters

Roll of florists' silver wire

Florists' scissors

Thick raffia plait; ours was 22in (55cm) long

Raffia

Open-weave ribbon 1½in (4cm) wide

Scissors

Selection of spices such as dried red chillies, nutmegs, cinnamon sticks and garlic

Selection of evergreen herbs such as bay, rosemary and sage

Fennel seedheads

Marjoram flowers

3 Cut a length of silver wire and thread 10–12 chillies on to it. Twist the wire ends to hold the chillies in a cluster.

4 Cut several stub wires in half and bend them into U-shaped staples. Cut short stems of the herb leaves, flowers and seeds, gather them into mixed bunches and bind the stems with silver wire. Fix the bunches at intervals along the plait by pressing in the staples.

5 Tie three or four cinnamon sticks into bundles with the raffia, tie a knot and cut off the ends. Push a stub wire staple through the raffia and fix the bundles to the plait. Wire the clusters of chillies, nutmegs and the garlic at intervals along the plait.

6 Finish the design with generous bows of the open-weave ribbon, wired through the back of the loops. Neaten the ends by cutting them slantwise.

Herbal Gift Rings

Make aromatic rings from fresh or dried herbs and present them as unusual and thoughtful gifts to cookery-loving friends. You can follow our example and use rosemary, purple sage and marjoram individually, or take several herbs together and perhaps include bay, fennel seedheads and others.

1 We used ready-made copper rings, but you could make them by joining two stub wires together to form a circle. You can, if you wish, bind the wire circles with gutta-percha tape before decorating them with the herbs.

YOU WILL NEED

Wire rings; ours were 7in (18cm) in diameter

Gutta-percha tape

Roll of fine silver wire

Scissors

Florists' scissors

Selection of ribbons

Rosemary leaves

Purple sage leaves

Marjoram flowers

2 Take several short stems of rosemary together, wrap them around the wire ring and bind them tightly with the roll wire. Add more stems and bind them on to the ring all the way around, until it is covered. Cover another ring with short sprays of purple sage leaves in a similar way.

3 The third ring is covered with mauve and white marjoram flowers. You can use fresh flowers and leave them to dry attractively on the ring, or use flowers which have aleady been dried. Finish each ring with a small, decorative bow of festive ribbon.

4 The herbal rings are shown as part of a culinary, and highly aromatic, gift basket. The rosemary ring is tied to the basket handle, the marjoram ring frames a pile of rosy apples, and the sage ring is in the foreground. Stems of dried fennel are grouped at the back of the basket.

Herb Wreath

To wander in a herb garden on a summer's evening, when all the myriad aromas are at their most pungent, is a delightful experience and one to savour. This colourful wreath can be composed of fresh materials and left to dry naturally, a nostalgic reminder of the scents of summer.

YOU WILL NEED

Flat copper-wire ring; ours was 10in (25cm) in diameter

Twine

Scissors

Florists' scissors

Stub wires

Dry sphagnum moss or you could use well-dried hay

Selection of herbs and cottage-garden flowers, such as purple sage, sage, marjoram, fennel, bunnies' ears *(Stachys lanata)*, cornflowers, modern pinks, love-in-a-mist flowers and seedheads, everlasting peas, lavender, veronica

1 Cover the ring thickly on both sides with the moss, binding it round and round with twine. The directions for covering a ring in this way are given on page 57. Our selection of herbs and flowers was in the purple, pink, wine-red and grey range, with touches of green for contrast.

2 Cut short the stems of the herbs and flowers, and form them into mixed bunches. If you plan to leave the decoration to dry, you will need more bunches, to allow them to diminish in size as the moisture evaporates. Bind the stems of each bunch with a stub wire and twist the ends tightly at the back.

3 To position the first bunch of herbs, push the wire into the moss and through to the back of the wreath. Twist it over the outer circle of the wire ring and bend it flat.

4 Arrange more bunches all around the ring, keeping them close together. Position them so that some flower heads face towards the inside of the wreath, and others face outwards. The design should have a jagged and uneven rather than a smooth outline.

5 The essence of summer – the completed ring composed of a colourful and shapely blend of herbs and traditional plants.

Golden Nut Ring

All that glitters may not be gold, but at Christmas time it is a valuable asset to have on the table. This decorative twig ring is embellished with gilded nuts and cones, and others in their natural state by way of attractive contrast. The design is almost unbelievably quick to make.

1 Choose the most decorative twig ring you can find or make your own. This one is in unbleached, twisted willow and has just the right kind of indentations and cavities needed to take the nuts. Make your selection of nuts as varied as possible.

YOU WILL NEED

Willow twig ring; ours was 10in (25cm) in diameter

Ozone-friendly gold aerosol spray

Clear, quick-setting, all-purpose glue

Ribbons, ½in (12mm) and 1¼in (3cm) wide

Scissors

Stub wires

Wire cutters

Selection of nuts, such as pecans, almonds, walnuts, chestnuts, brazils

Small pine cones

2 Cover the working surface with paper and select the nuts and cones to be gilded. Spray them on one side, leave them to dry, then turn them over and spray them on the other side. Leave them to dry again.

3 Squeeze a generous amount of glue onto the base of each nut and cone, press it onto the ring and hold it in place for a few moments while the glue sets. Alternate the sprayed materials with the natural ones to achieve a good colour balance.

4 Cut two lengths of the narrower ribbon. Cut a stub wire in half, wrap it around the centre of the ribbons, and press the ends of the wire into the ring. Make a bow from the wider ribbon, bend half a stub wire into a U-shape, thread it through the loop at the back of the bow, and fix it to the ring.

5 The warm and glistening colours on this decorative twig ring are certainly an asset to a dining table.

Berry Garland

An evergreen garland studded with true or false berries makes a seasonal decoration for a footed plate, a pedestal dish or a compote. The dish could display an arrangement of pomanders and nuts, the Christmas cake, or the Christmas pudding.

1 Cut a length of wire to go around the circumference of the dish and, if you like, make a hook and eye at the ends. Glossy evergreens are the best choice for a decorative garland of this kind. We contrasted dark, heavily veined ivy leaves with suitably slender sprays of lighter green box.

YOU WILL NEED

Pedestal dish

Thick wire

Roll of fine silver wire

Ribbon ¼in (6mm) wide

Sprays of evergreens, such as ivy and box

False berries

2 It's a horticultural phenomenon: sprays of box resplendent with glowing red berries. Wind several berries onto each evergreen spray so that they make a real impact.

3 Using the roll wire, bind ivy and box sprays together onto the wire ring. Bind successive sprays so that they cover the stems of the ones before. Continue binding on more evergreens all around the ring until it is completely covered.

4 Cut off a length of ribbon to make a bow. Cut the remainder into three equal lengths and, using them together, bind them over and around the evergreens, leaving the ribbons loose, so that they make gentle folds. Tie the ribbon ends where they meet, and cover the join with a ribbon bow.

5 Fix the evergreen garland over the dish and cut off any stray stems or prominent leaves that look out of place.

Kissing Ring

A kissing ring of evergreens combined with berry-bright fruits is a traditional decoration to hang over the table or in the hall at Christmas time. Here it is interpreted with "designer" fruits, but it could equally well be made with small rosy apples or with satsumas.

1 Long trails of ivy are the perfect choice to make the evergreen wreath because they can so easily be twined around the ring. The fruits we chose were artificial apples and (not quite in scale) equally bright strawberries.

YOU WILL NEED

Twisted-twig ring; ours was 12in (30cm) in diameter

Tape measure

Stub wires

Wire cutters

Florists' scissors

Ribbon 1½in (4cm) wide

Scissors

Pin, safety-pin or staples

Trails of ivy

Real or artificial fruits

2 Measure the circumference of the ring to ascertain the distance between each fruit. If the fruit has a hanging loop, as ours had, it is simple to hang it on a stub-wire hook. Cut a stub wire in half, bend it into a U-shape, push it through the loop and insert the two ends of the wire in the underside of the ring.

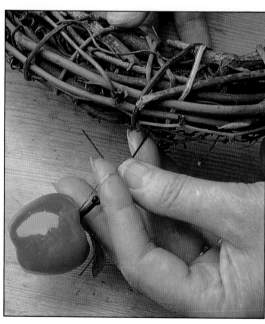

3 Wind trails of ivy around the twig ring, taking them over and over the ring. Secure each stem end with a bent stub-wire staple. Check that the ivy is evenly distributed, and bind on extra trails or staple in individual leaves if there are gaps.

4 Tie a short length of ribbon around the twig ring, making a double knot at the top. Thread a long piece of ribbon through it, to hang the decoration. Repeat this twice more.

5 Make four ribbon bows, three to fix to the ring and one to fix at the top. Attach, using bent stub-wire staples.

6 Join the six ends of ribbon hangings at the top (you could use a pin, safety-pin, or staples), and fix the decoration where it is to hang. Attach the fourth ribbon bow at the top.

Children's Candy Ring

Here's a ring that will bring a sparkle to the children's eyes! And older children will delight in helping to make it. Perhaps it is worth noting that the candies have been counted – there are four in each paper-doily cone!

YOU WILL NEED

Large flat plate

Small shallow dish

Block of absorbent foam

Knife

String

Scissors

6 paper doilies, 7½in (19cm) in diameter

Stub wires

Wire cutters

Florists' scissors

Ribbons ½in (12mm) wide

Sprays of evergreen, such as juniper or cypress

Brightly wrapped candies

1 Outline the flat plate with slices of soaked absorbent foam and tie around the foam with string. Choose evergreens that have a feathery outline. The one shown is juniper.

2 Make a cone shape from each of the paper doilies. Fold a doily into half, and half again, to give a quarter segment, and then pinch the cone to make a point. Wrap half a stub wire tightly around the point.

3 Arrange the doilies evenly around the ring, pushing the wire into the foam. Ease out the paper to make full, open cone shapes. Cut short sprays of evergreen and insert them into the foam, between the doilies, until all the spaces are filled and the foam blocks are completely hidden.

4 Cut the stub wires in half and twist one around the wrappings of each of the candies. Fill the paper cones with candies by pushing the wires through the holes on the doilies.

5 Cut equal lengths of ribbons, wrap half a stub wire around the centre and push the wire into the foam. Cut the ribbon ends slantwise. Fill the dish in the centre of the design with more candies. As the wires do not pierce the candies at all, the goodies will be safe to eat when the design is dismantled.

Special Occasions

At times of celebration and re-joicing, it seems only natural to express a sense of occasion through flowers. Whether it is a yearly event such as Christmas, or a once-in-a-lifetime occasion such as a wedding, swathes of flowers are the surest way to convey the festive feeling. Floral decorations can speak of new life at Easter or love and romance on Valentine's Day; they can welcome guests and family at Christmas and New Year. Even the most impromptu of parties is an opportunity to deck tables with floral ornaments. If you need to transform your home or garden into a gala setting, stunning effects can be created with remarkably little effort by using these designs to add a touch of glamour.

Many of the designs in this section are

unashamedly traditional, interpretations of decorations that have become an essential part of celebrations all around the world. Red and green, for instance, are the colours that evoke Christmas – so what better choice for a front door wreath? We no longer believe, as people did in ancient times, that evergreen trees have magical powers (since they retain their leaves when other trees are bare). But we do appreciate the way holly, ivy, cypress and mistletoe transform our homes for the festive season.

A wedding would hardly seem like a wedding without flowers, nor a bride a bride without a bouquet. These designs are soft and romantic, avoiding harsh formality. Adapt the flowers suggested here to suit your own colour scheme.

ABOVE *When you're giving a midsummer night's dream of a party, these Flower Torches (page 172) are the brightest decorative idea around.*

Easter Table Ring

Flickering tapers and a "nest" of eggs set the scene for this pretty Easter table centrepiece.

YOU WILL NEED

Large flat plate

Small shallow dish

Block of absorbent foam

Knife

String

Scissors

Florists' scissors

6 thin tapers

Eggs

Moss

Varigated leaves, such as periwinkle

Alstroemeria (Peruvian lilies)

Spray carnations

Freesias

QUICK FOAM RINGS

This is a quick and easy way to make a foam circle when you do not have, or cannot obtain, a pre-formed foam ring. You can use a block of dry foam in a similar way to make a dried flower table ring.

1 Making a ring of absorbent foam (slices cut from a dry block) requires a flat plate to form the base of the design, and a shallow dish to hold the moss and eggs.

2 Cut the foam block into slices 1¼in (3cm) wide. Cut each slice in half across the width, and trim off the top and bottom corners.

151

3 Soak the foam pieces in water for several minutes. Arrange them around the plate and tie a piece of string around the outside of the foam blocks to hold them in place. Put a handful of moss in the dish.

4 Start building up the design by positioning short sprays of the foliage around the inner and outer rims of the foam circle, so that the leaves overlap the edges. Cut short the stems of the alstroemeria (Peruvian lilies) and position them to face inwards and outwards.

5 Turn the plate round, complete the ring with one colour of alstroemeria (Peruvian lilies), then add the second colour. Again, face the flowers alternate ways, with some overlapping the rims of the plate and dish.

6 Fill the design with spray carnations, their stems cut short and the flower heads resting close against the foam. Arrange the brightest flowers, in this case the yellow freesias, at intervals. Check that there are no gaps in the design and that no foam shows through at all.

7 Cut each taper into two pieces of uneven lengths. Use the knife to scrape away the wax from the top of each of the lower pieces, to expose a short length of the wick. Press the tapers into the foam to form a cluster at one end of the design.

8 Arrange a few eggs on the moss in the centre of the floral ring. These could, if you wish, be painted or dyed. Have some more tapers ready to replace the first batch as they burn down, and watch that they do not burn too close to the flowers.

Easter Basket

Use "plain" eggs for a natural effect, painted or stencilled eggs for a more lavish look. Keep extra ornament simple though, so that it does not become too fussy.

1 The basket is filled with moss, a safe nest for the eggs.

YOU WILL NEED

Shallow basket

Medium-gauge stub wires

Eggs

Sphagnum moss

Pink rhodanthe

Pink sea lavender

Pink helichrysums (strawflowers)

Poppy seedheads

Purple marjoram flowers

Lavender

2 A posy composed of pink rhodanthe, pink sea lavender and helichrysums (strawflowers). The stems are bound with a stub wire.

3 Two of the posies – they need not be identical – are attached to the basket rim, the ends of the stub wires pressed between the woven slats. The head of one posy covers and conceals the stems of the one before.

4 The basket rim is covered with a ring of posies, the round shapes of the everlasting flowers contrasting effectively with the lace-like stems of sea lavender.

5 When it is filled with eggs, the basket makes an eye-catching centrepiece for the Easter table.

Candle Garlands

Plain white candles are transformed into the prettiest of Easter decorations with a ring of pastel flowers and trailing ribbons.

1 We chose plain white "altar" candles, but you could decorate small white household candles, or ones in various colours, in a similar way. As you need only a few flowers, you could use snippings left over from larger designs, making the garlands to match a table centre or wall decoration.

YOU WILL NEED

Plain white candles; ours were 12in (30cm) long and 1in (2.5cm) in diameter

Roll of fine silver wire

Scissors

Florists' scissors

Short lengths of satin ribbon, ¾in (2cm) wide

Freesias

Alstroemeria (Peruvian lilies)

Spray carnations

Spray chrysanthemums

Gypsophila (baby's breath)

2 Bind the silver wire round the candle and secure it. Place a few flowers on the candle and bind the stems with the wire. Position more flowers close to the first ones, and bind the wire round the stems to secure them. Continue until the candle is encircled by flowers, and secure the wire.

3 Bind the ribbon once round the candle to cover the wire, and tie it in a double knot, leaving the ends trailing. Cut the ends slantwise to neaten them.

4 The finished candle garlands. Spray the flowers with cool water to keep them fresh. They can look equally good on a dining table or a sideboard table.

Halloween Candle Ring

Candles are crucial to the atmosphere created for a Halloween party. We have designed a candlestick ring composed of dried materials in weird and wonderful shapes, from spiky cereals to prickly flower heads, and in an improbable mixture of colours, taking in both mauve and orange.

1 As all the dried materials are used with short lengths of stem, and as the colour scheme is random rather than carefully planned, you should be able to use snippings left over from other designs. Try to include some rugged shapes, such as the thistles and carthamus.

CANDLE CARE

Take care that the candles do not burn down too close to the dried materials. Do not leave the lighted decoration in a room where young children or animals are left unattended.

2 If you cannot obtain a dry foam ring, you can cut one from a block of foam, using a small plate for the outline. Cut two semi-circles, butt them together and tie them around with string. Insert short lengths of oat stems around the top and outside of the ring. The inside of the ring is not decorated.

3 Fill in the design with flowers in random order. Cut some stems very short and press the flower head close against the foam. That way, you need fewer flowers to cover and conceal it.

4 The completed ring, with heads of wheat and stems of oats shooting off in all directions and the foam ring covered with a kaleidoscope of colour. This ring is cut so that the candlestick just rests on top of it.

5 A trio of lighting effects, with stubby red candles pressed into the top of rosy red apples (an appropriate idea for Halloween) and a night-light owl beaming approval.

Advent Ring

The tradition in the Christian church, of lighting one candle on each of the four Sundays of Advent, is brought into the home with this ring, composed of winter-green, white and silver dried materials.

1 Unusually, this design uses an absorbent foam ring, unsoaked, instead of a dry foam one, with mainly dried flowers. Cut the sea lavender, honesty, and mistletoe into short sprays, and make bunches of the white ammobium, wrapping the short stems with half a stub wire.

YOU WILL NEED

Absorbent foam ring; ours was 10in (25cm) in diameter

Stub wires

Wire cutters

4 plastic candle-holding spikes

Ribbon 1¼in (3cm) wide

4 candles

Florists' scissors

Dried sea lavender

Dried honesty

Mistletoe

Dried ammobium

2 Press the candle spikes into the foam at equal distances around the ring. Tie a ribbon around the base of the ring, to partially conceal it. The knot in the ribbon will be covered by the decorative bow.

3 Arrange short sprays of sea lavender all around the ring so that it extends over the inner and outer rims. The sea lavender serves as a background against which the other more high-profile materials will be seen.

MAKING CANDLE SPIKES

It is not advisable to press thick candles (the ones in our design are 1in (2.5cm) in diameter) directly into the foam, as they may break it up. If you cannot obtain the type of candle spikes we show, you can make "stilts" of matchsticks or cocktail sticks to support the candle and press into the foam. Tape four sticks around the base of each candle, leaving about 1in (2.5cm) extending beneath it. Push the matchsticks into the foam so that the candle just rests on the surface.

4 Fill the design with short sprays of honesty and mistletoe, and bunches of ammobium. Turn the ring round and check that there are no gaps which allow the foam to show through. If there are, add more sprays. Make a bow from the contrasting ribbon. Bend half a stub wire into a U-shape and push it through the loop at the back of the bow. Press the wire into the foam ring so that the bow covers the knot in the encircling ribbon.

Welcome Wreath

A colourful wreath of evergreens and other natural materials hanging on the front door gives a warm welcome to guests through Christmas and the New Year.

1 Cover the wire ring thickly on both sides with hay or moss. The method is described on page 57. Select short, full sprays of evergreens to give a variety of leaf shape and texture, and include some high-gloss materials, such as holly or ivy, to give the design sparkle.

2 To make a hook for hanging, bend a stub wire to make a circular shape in the centre, and twist the two ends beneath it. Push the two ends of the wire into the wreath and twist them round the outer ring of the wire frame. The hook will be covered by the evergreens at the top of the design.

3 Attach all the materials, even the evergreen sprays, to wires before inserting them in the wreath. Twist half a stub wire around each stem, leaving a false stalk to insert in the wreath. Wrap a stub wire around the lowest ring of scales on each cone and twist it underneath. Cut the cinnamon sticks in half, wrap them around the centre with a stub wire and tie raffia to cover it.

YOU WILL NEED

Flat copper-wire ring

Stub wires

Wire cutters

Florists' scissors

Raffia

Ribbon 1¼in (3cm) wide

Scissors

Well-dried hay or sphagnum moss

Selection of evergreens

Dried poppyheads

Small pine cones

Cinnamon sticks

4 Push the wired materials into and through the wreath and bend the wire stalk over at the back, so that it is held firm against the wire ring frame.

Build up the design so that the poppyheads, cinnamon sticks and cones are evenly distributed around the ring.

5 Tie two ribbon bows, one with long trailing ends for the top of the wreath and the other flat. Bend half a stub wire in a U-shape, push it through the loop of the back of each bow, and insert it in the wreath. Neaten the ends of the ribbon by cutting them into inverted V-shapes.

6 This beautiful wreath is the ideal way to put visitors at their ease, especially hanging against a lovely wooden door.

Valentine Heart

The perfect gift for your partner on Valentine's Day, a wedding anniversary or a birthday, or just to say, "I love you". The design is composed on a heart-shaped twig ring and decorated with the most romantic of all floral symbols, red roses.

1 You may be able to buy a heart-shaped twisted-twig ring at a florist or flower club. If not, you could make one by forming a length of thick wire into a heart shape and covering it with supple twigs.

YOU WILL NEED

Heart-shaped twisted-twig ring

Roll of fine silver wire

Scissors

Stub wires

Wire cutters

Florists' scissors

Lacy ribbon; ours was 2in (5cm)

Wide cotton crochet

Dried rosebuds

Dried sea lavender

Dried gypsophila (baby's breath)

2 Cut short the stems of the dried flowers and make them into posies, composed of two rosebuds and a few sprays of sea lavender and gypsophila (baby's breath). Bind the posy stems with roll wire. Cut stub wires in half and bend them into U-shaped staples.

3 Place a posy flat against the twig shape, with the stems following the outline. Secure the posy by pushing a wire staple over the stems and into the twigs.

4 Add more posies to follow the heart shape, positioning them so that the flowers of one posy cover and hide the stems of the one before. Reverse the direction of the stems at the base of the heart, so that all the flower heads are facing towards the top of the design. Our design includes two posies featuring cream instead of red rosebuds – just to be different.

5 Tie the lacy ribbon into a bow and trim the ends neatly. Push a wire staple through the loop at the back, and press it into the top centre of the heart.

6 The finished heart – designed to melt your heart.

Bridesmaid's Hoop

These hoops are easier for small flower girls and nervous bridemaids to carry than bouquets. Our design is composed of mainly yellow and white flowers with pretty entwined ribbons.

YOU WILL NEED

Length of bent cane to form a hoop

Strong adhesive tape, such as insulating tape

White gutta-percha tape or narrow ribbon for binding

Scissors

Ribbon ¾in (2cm) wide

Roll of fine silver wire

Florists' scissors

Alstroemeria (Peruvian lilies)

Spray chrysanthemums

Spray carnations

Freesias

1 Bent cane is an ideal material to make a carrying hoop. We made a hoop 16in (40cm) in diameter from a cane 56in (142cm) long. The flowers we chose are specially long-lasting, and therefore well suited to being without a moisture source.

2 Join the two ends of the cane by butting them together and binding them together with strong adhesive tape. Cover the cane circle with gutta-percha tape or with narrow ribbon. While the tape stays firmly in place, ribbon does not. Pull it tightly at every turn to get a neat, even finish.

3 Leaving one long end at the top of the bow, wind the ribbon loosely around the hoop so that it forms decorative curves. Tie the two ends into a bow and trim the ends by cutting them across diagonally.

4 Divide the flowers into twelve groups of different types and colours. With the roll wire, bind one group to the cane so that the flower heads wrap around it. Reverse the stems of the next group, position them over the others, and bind them in place.

5 Bind on more groups of flowers, always in pairs so that the stems overlap and are concealed by the flower heads. Tie the ribbon bow at the base of the design, over the cane and the stems of two flower groups, and trim the ends. Spray the flowers with a fine mist of cool water.

6 All ready, complete with dainty lace goves, for the young bridesmaid to carry. When a design is in two main colours, it can be interesting and effective to add small amounts of a third shade – in this case, the pink of the alstroemeria (Peruvian lilies).

PREPARING AHEAD

It may be more convenient for you to make the design to a part-way stage and assemble it just before the wedding. To do this, bind the cane hoop and bind on the ribbon, to the end of Step 3. Divide the flowers into twelve groups and bind the stems of each group with roll wire to make a posy. Stand the posies in water until you are ready to complete the design. Then unwire each posy in turn, so that the flowers can be arranged to wrap around the cane and bind them in place.

Floral Wedding Ring

Created in colours to blend with those worn by the bridal party, this flower ring could decorate the table in the vestry, or the bride's table at the wedding reception. The addition of gypsophila (baby's breath) creates a veil-like effect which is specially suited to the occasion.

YOU WILL NEED

Absorbent foam ring, 10in (25cm) in diameter

Florists' scissors

Sprays of light evergreen leaves, such as box

Spray chrysanthemums

Roses

Modern pinks

Sweet peas

Gypsophila (baby's breath)

1 Place the flowers and foliage in cool water before arranging them. This will help to prolong their freshness. Soak the absorbent foam ring in water for several minutes until it is completely saturated.

2 Cut short the evergreen sprays and arrange them around the inner and outer rims of the foam ring, trailing downwards so that they mask the base. Position other sprays around the top of the ring, where they will alternate with the flowers and give a natural look to the design.

3 Cut short the stems of the spray chrysanthemums and position them, some facing inwards and some outwards, around the ring. You can use the flower buds, too, to give variety of size and shape.

4 Place the roses, the largest of the flowers used, at equal intervals around the ring. Fill in the design with pinks and sweet peas, balancing the colours more or less equally. Turn the ring around and check that there are no gaps and that the foam and base are completely concealed. If not, add a few more sprays of foliage or flowers.

5 Cut sprays of gypsophila (baby's breath) and trim off any wayward stems. Position the sprays around the ring so that they come just above the other flowers and partially obscure them, like a veil. Spray the flowers with a fine mist of cool water.

6 This floral wedding ring, created in pastel tints of pink and blue, would be a pretty decoration for a summer wedding. To tone with other bridal colour schemes, it could be composed of peach-coloured roses, apricot-coloured sweet peas and cream spray carnations, or yellow roses, blue cornflowers and cream spray chrysanthemums.

Bridal Headdress

There's a special pride in composing a bridal headdress for a member of your family or for a friend. This simple style, a circlet of sweet peas and spray carnations, would be charming both for a young bride and her bridesmaids.

YOU WILL NEED

2 stub wires or length of medium-gauge wire

White gutta-percha tape

Scissors

Roll of fine silver wire

Florists' scissors

Velvet ribbon 1in (2.5cm) wide

Sweet peas

Spray carnations

Gypsophila (baby's breath)

1 Flowers for a bridal headdress are chosen in colours to complement the bridesmaids' dresses and the overall colour scheme of the wedding – in this case pink and cream. You can use similar flowers to tone with a mauve and blue, red and white, or blue and yellow theme. Stand the flowers in water.

CO-ORDINATED TABLE DECORATIONS

For an attractive and co-ordinated look, you could use similar flowers and an identical colour scheme to make floral ring decorations for the guests' and bridal tables.

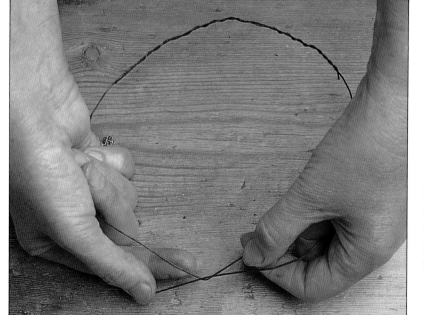

2 To make a circlet from stub wires, twist the ends of two wires together, bend them into a circle, and twist the other two ends together. Or you can make the core from a single piece of wire. For a circlet 7in (18cm) in diameter you will need a piece of wire 22in (55cm) long.

3 Bind the wire circle with gutta-percha tape, slightly overlapping each binding with the one before. Make small, short-stemmed posies of mixed flowers, including a few sweet peas, a spray carnation and a spray or two of gypsophila (baby's breath). Bind the stems with roll wire and trim the stem ends.

4 Place one end of the posies against the wire circlet and bind it on by taking the roll wire round and round the wire and stems. Without breaking off the roll wire, bind on the next posy so that the flowers cover the stems of the one before. Work around the ring in this way, leaving a small gap for the ribbon bow.

5 Velvet ribbon has an especially luxurious look and holds its shape well. Tie the ribbon around the circlet, tie a bow and arrange it to follow the lines of the ring. Trim the ribbon ends neatly.

6 Spray the headdress with a fine mist of cool water, and keep it in a cool place (even the refrigerator) until the moment it is needed.

Flower Torches

This pair of unbelievably simple-to-make floral torches can decorate the garden, the patio, the porch, conservatory, wherever appropriate. You can "plant" the canes in a flower bed, in pots and tubs, anywhere you want to introduce some colour and create a sensation.

1 Mark the centre of each of the foam cylinders to ensure that you position them centrally on the cane. Soak the cylinders in water for several minutes until they are completely soaked. Working over a waterproof surface, push each cylinder in turn on to the cane.

YOU WILL NEED

For each torch:

Bamboo cane, about 42in (107cm) long

4 cylinders of absorbent foam

Stub wires

Florists' scissors

Strips of different coloured paper ribbon

Selection of long-lasting flowers in white and bright colours, such as feverfew, cornflowers, single roses, campion *(Lychnis coronaria)*, santolina

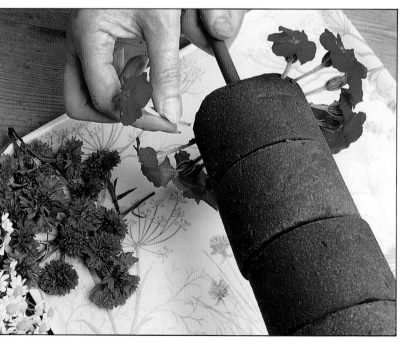

2 The top cylinder should be level with the top of the cane. Bind a stub wire round the cane to keep them from slipping. Cut the stems of the flowers short and to equal lengths. Position the first row of flowers around the base of the lowest foam cylinder, keeping the flowers close together.

3 Continue making the rings of flowers all the way up the foam. Small examples, such as feverfew (shown here) may be gathered into bunches and several stems inserted together.

4 With rings and rings of flowers in red, white, blue, and yellow covering the foam, finish off the design with something of a floral flourish on top. You could use a spray of single roses or a dome of feverfew, the stems cut to graduated lengths.

5 Gather up streamers of paper ribbon in different colours and wrap them around the cane, just below the foam. Fix them in place by wrapping a stub wire around the cane. The lowest ring of flowers will conceal the wire.

6 You can "plant" the torches in a nearly-all-green part of the garden, in a flower bed, in pots and tubs – anywhere you want to introduce some colour and create a sensation.

7 The finished flower torches can also be positioned on either side of a porch, doorway or outside staircase.

INDEX